WE LIVE WITH OUR EYES OPEN

WE LIVE WITH OUR EYES OPEN

DOM HUBERT
VAN ZELLER

THE CENACLE PRESS
AT SILVERSTREAM PRIORY

First Published 1949, by Sheed and Ward, London.

This edition republished 2023 by Silverstream Priory
with the kind permission of Downside Abbey.
New material and graphic design copyright
© 2023 by Silverstream Priory.

All rights reserved:
No part of this book may be reproduced or transmitted,
in any form or by any means, without permission.

The Cenacle Press at Silverstream Priory
Silverstream Priory
Stamullen, County Meath, K32 T189, Ireland
www.cenaclepress.com

Nihil Obstat:
Patricius Morris, S.T.D., L.S.S. censor deputatus
Imprimatur:
E. Morrogh Bernard, Vic. Gen. Westmonasteri,
die 22a Januarii, 1949

Nihil Obstat:
Dom Cyprian Gibson, O.S.B., Censor Cong.
Imprimatur:
Dom Herbert Byrne, O.S.B., Ab. Pres.

ppr 9781915544360

Cover art:
Claude Monet, The Church at Varengeville (1882).
Cover design by Julian Kwasniewski
Interior design by Michael Schrauzer.

To
GORDON McNABB
by way of resuming a correspondence

*Though life may be a gift horse
Presented to the race,
We have to go on being told
To look it in the face.*

CONTENTS

What Spiritual Writers Call Creatures 1

Jealousy 5

Truth 15

Personal Influence 23

More About Creatures 27

Leadership 33

Taking the Smooth with the Rough 40

Bitterness 44

Integrity 48

Sex 51

Interior Prayer: Its Expression 57

Interior Prayer: Its Material 61

Interior Prayer: Its Problem 65

Interior Prayer: Its Condition 69

Interior Prayer: Its Idiom 74

Love In General 78

Married Love 84

Married Life 90

Mainly For Schoolmasters 100

More About Education 106

Father Bede Jarrett 112

The Mass 129

The Mass and Marriage 133

The Challenge	137
Approach to Mysticism	142
Mysticism in Operation	145
The Mystic's Charity	150
Approach to Asceticism	154
Asceticism in Operation	159
The Ascetic's Charity	163
Sensitiveness	168
The Modern Gospel	173
They Didn't Look Away	176
The Ends of Chapters	187
The Show Goes On	193
Holy Saturday	197
Our Lady's Sorrows	203
The Good News of the Gospel	207
We Live With Our Eyes Open	210

WHAT SPIRITUAL WRITERS CALL CREATURES

IN A LETTER FROM SHELLEY TO Gisborne there occurs this passage: "I think one is always in love with something or other; the error—and I confess it is not easy for spirits cased in flesh and blood to avoid it—consists in not seeing in a mortal image the likeness of what is perhaps eternal." The "perhaps" is the only word in the statement that is not entirely happy, because if the thing sought is something real and right and God-ordered and therefore beautiful, it is certainly, and not perhaps, a reflexion of the Divine. As far as this world goes it is an absolute, not a probable. But it is a likeness, nevertheless, and not the reality itself. It is in seeing creatures as likenesses, true but inadequate likenesses, that the whole difficulty consists. How to find in our loves the essence and object of our charity is precisely Shelley's problem. It is not primarily a question of combining the two loves—love of God and love of creatures—or even of finding a synthesis which works out more or less satisfactorily in practice; it is a question of seeing love as a whole. It is taking Shelley's "mortal images" *as* images and not as unrelated entities. To look at life in such a way, or rather to look *through* life in such a way, requires more than merely deciding to concentrate on the derivative quality of created beauty. It supposes a habit of mind which can be found and built up only in prayer. Reading helps; association with people who are holy helps; but to be able to combine the detachment necessary for high spirituality with the love due to creatures as expressions of the Creator is a work of grace which normally prayer alone discovers for us.

Notice that Shelley says we are always in love with something or other. There would be nothing the matter with this if it were not for the fact that love is, proverbially, blind. Love can't, unless the habit of mind which we have spoken of is present, see beyond the creature. We may, to quote Shelley's words, be spirits cased in flesh and blood, but the trouble is that flesh and blood falls more easily and perceptibly in love than does the spirit, and flesh and blood perceives flesh and blood: nothing more. Inform flesh and blood with grace, give to the spirit its controlling power, establish the right order in the soul, and that which is terrestrial sees through with the eye of faith to that which is heavenly. Sees through, moreover, not as one who peeps through a gap in a curtain and is granted a reward for his search, but rather as one who becomes more and more aware of the light behind the curtain shining through. To the saints, of course, so clear is this vision of the light that the curtain in between is almost wholly transparent, and an effort has even to be made sometimes to get the perspective. Which only shows that while we are still in this life our gaze is always liable to be either longsighted or shortsighted: it's almost impossible to get the focus dead right. Until our eyes are trained to behold the Beatific Vision, there must always be a margin for the kind of error suggested in the quotation. The margin, however, can be reduced to the minimum, and the mortal can be loved without prejudice to the eternal. Further, because loved rightly, the mortal is loved more deeply and really. All this in virtue of prayer, in virtue of the orientation of heart which is the outcome of prayer.

"It sounds too easy for words," you will say; "I have only to pray, and the problem of rival loyalties will melt into thin air . . . I Shall find myself loving God and people all in one." Such is the theory. "Love God," said St. Augustine, "and do what you will." But even so it is, in practice, uncommonly difficult to keep the balance. Before long we begin to fool ourselves that we are loving God when in fact we are concerned with doing what we will. Right through life, or at all events until the soul is far advanced in sanctity and can comfortably keep creatures in their place, there will always be the temptation to render to Caesar the things that are God's. More perhaps as we grow older in the spiritual life, and are able to take creatures in our stride without gross distraction, does this temptation present itself. We begin to feel safe in the new mode of their enjoyment, we have accepted them as God's utterance and are duly grateful, we have derived help instead of suffering hurt (as was the case before) from their presence in our lives . . . and we get careless. It ought not to be so difficult for us to see when we are snatching at, delaying in, holding on to the things of this world at the expense of our grasp of those things which belong to the next. Yet so great is the power of self-deception that we can never be absolutely sure. The human judgment is more liable to go wrong when called upon to decide what is and what is not an inordinate attachment of the heart than in almost any other decision which it is expected to make. Considering how much depends upon the answer to this precise question, we must insure at least a right approach to it. Does not the obscurity sometimes arise because we are applying the wrong sort of tests? Because we are trying to force the practical intellect to manoeuvre on a ground which is more spiritual than physical? We should realise that there are regions beyond which common sense and even psychology cannot take us; it is in prayer that the undefined frontiers of attachment are learned. There are things in the spiritual life which we cannot follow on a map or learn out of a book: we come to get the feel of them indirectly, by the fact of responding to grace. If we approach the creatures which we are doubtful about and challenge them face to face, we find ourselves beginning to wonder whether the answering voice was not disguised; it is a safer plan to get up into the heavens and look down. At least we shall be looking at the world more from the angle of Him who created it.

JEALOUSY

ONCE IN A BUS I HEARD ONE young woman ask another what was her favourite tune. "Fancy asking," was the reply; "why, it's *Jealousy* of course." It was the "of course" which puzzled me; I wondered what the melody could be like which should call forth such a prompt appreciation. Months later I heard it on the air, rendered by the theatre organ, and the scene in the bus came back to me: how the girl whose favourite composition it was had leaned back and closed her eyes (the better, presumably, to turn over its associations in the memory), and how I had vaguely hoped, as Edgware Road flashed by, that she would hum a bar or two so that I might share its savour. So this was *Jealousy*. That young woman's favourite composition. Well, well, well. It wasn't mine, that's all. Though not caring much for *Jealousy* as a tune, I do rather care for it as a theme. In a sense it is my favourite vice.

In the first place, jealousy must not be confused with envy. We can be envious of another's talents, another's wealth, another's looks, chances, success and so on, but if we are *jealous* we have an eye on another's affection—and this causes far more trouble. An envious person may be an uneasy person, never satisfied and often consumed with self-pity, but a jealous person is made miserable; jealousy is far more harrowing, far more unbalancing, than envy. A jealous person is made suspicious, furtive, morose, unreasonable. Jealousy is the most hideously withering evil: it finds a rose-tree and leaves a stick. Not only is jealousy far worse than envy for the individual concerned, but it is also far worse for everyone else. Envy seldom gets beyond the stage of wanting what it hasn't got, and even if it goes to the full length of getting what it wants by underhand means it never reaches the appropriate activity of jealousy—which is to poison the sources of love.

Jealous people are of two kinds: those who know their jealousy to be unjustified, spoiling, a waste of something good, and disastrous to the course of love of which it is the disordered growth; and those who don't. The first kind can be cured of their evil; the second, but for a very special grace from God, can't. In both cases jealousy amounts almost to a disease: it spreads rapidly, it infects, it isolates, it calls for the knife. Since anything which is written here will have not the smallest effect upon the second type of jealous person mentioned above, we can confine ourselves to dealing with the first.

There are many forms which jealousy can take, and many stages in its development. As a rule it begins with such subtlety that we can live with it for a time without seeing through its disguise. Perhaps if we were quicker to detect it we would take more drastic steps to get rid of it; perhaps if we faced it the moment we felt it we would not fall back upon the excuse that some people are by nature more jealous than others. It is in the devil's interest that such an evil should not declare itself openly until it has got a hold, until it has become part of our character. Having got its hold, it races us off our feet and makes us more and more unreasonable about the one subject which calls for cool judgment before anything else.

How does the ordinary person *become* jealous? What is it that leads an uncomplicated nature into the twists and searchings of motive which are inseparable from this vice? What happens is often this. A man starts in all sincerity by believing that the pain which is caused by the other's straying affection — or supposed straying affection — is simply due to altruistic concern: he is interested in the other's good. Why not? He sees new enjoyments, new people, new openings coming into a life of which up till now he had seemed to possess the monopoly. "I wonder if it's wise; I don't like it." No suggestion of his own possessiveness; no hint of personal resentment. Jealousy begins by appearing to be objective. Soon the direction veers towards self, and the next stage is: "My influence is weakening, and mine was a better influence than anyone else's." The note of reproach has come in — which means that from now onwards the effort to counter other influences will be plaintive and appealing. There is, as yet, no admission of rivalry or talk of competition; there are assumptions of rights, however, and expressions of disapproval. Perhaps not until he says "I don't count any more" does the jealous man become aware of his spoiling tendency. Even then he may not recognise it fully as an evil, as material for sin. Feeling the sting of it, the sufferer imagines that his love is being martyred. Dramatising the whole thing, he sees a certain forlorn nobility in being rejected, he thinks how thankless has been his devotion. See how all this turns towards self: there is little real thought about the other person, little generosity. So subtle is the temptation that a man may canonise his jealousy, attributing it to the almost sacred character of his love: "If my affection were not so upright, I would not care as much as I do."

When, in finding ourselves to be neglected in favour of new friends, we pretend that our real agony is caused not by the sense of emptiness at all but by a fear for another's well-being and happiness, we need to look very closely indeed at the quality of that fear. To watch the wrecking of something beautiful is indeed an agony, but before we can claim that this experience is ours — before we range ourselves on the side of our Lady and the holy women at the foot of the Cross — let us make quite certain that what is beautiful is being wrecked . . . and not that we are imagining this so as to give colour to our resentment. Perhaps it is ourselves who are responsible for the process of wrecking: there is nothing that eats away at a relationship so surely as jealousy. The noblest affection can hardly be expected to stand up indefinitely against the wear of this rotting and querulous infirmity.

"You tell me I've fanned it up in my imagination," objects the sufferer, "but I can trace a deterioration in the one I love. New loyalties have brought about a change for the worse in all sorts of things: in outlook, taste, behaviour. I know I'm right." Even allowing that this is true, there is no possible good to be got out of either showing, or allowing oneself to feel, jealousy. To indulge this particular emotion can only lead to harm: it brings into the relationship an element which rules out any idea of reciprocal confidence. Insignificant acts are charged with meaning, and then misinterpreted. Slights are seen everywhere, and where they are not seen they are imagined — swollen out of all plausibility and backed up by trivial little bits of evidence recalled from the remote past. Reason is submerged; emotion is on top. Panics, suspicions, memories, doubts, nerves, willies of every sort.

One of the troubles about jealousy is that it leaves us no rest: it is a whole time occupation. All day and a large part of the night we are wondering what is going on in the life of the other person. We remember the attraction which was first exercised upon us, and we visualise the effect which it must be having in our absence. That the charm should be expressed at all is one thing which hurts us desperately; and that it should be responded to is something which hurts us even more. Dreading a thousand possibilities, we jump at a chance of finding out what has now become a secret: at all costs we must know what happens behind our back. "When I'm not there," we say, "your life is a closed book to me." If we can't get what we want by direct questioning, we resort to rather sly investigation, both being a flat denial of the trust which is the first condition of two people being able to get on together. How are the affections distributed? How is the time being spent? What are the guarantees for the future? If I could only get a promise which I could rely upon...

With snowball momentum the affair rolls out of control. Assurances of undying devotion are asked for — either by leading up to them with such a display of silent misery that enquiries are made as to what it is all about, or else by downright demands for a declaration — and are no sooner given than they are disbelieved. This, surely, is one of the chief miseries attaching to the evil of jealousy — that nothing is *believed* any more. There is no faith. And all the time the very thing that is most yearned for is certainty. Certainty about the past, the present, and the future. Certainty that everything is all right and that the affection is still possessed. But to the jealous man no amount of reassurances can possibly reassure; he is entrenched behind his doubt; he expects to be deceived; he sees himself always in the role of the poor duped idiot whose tragedy it has been to love a person incapable of returning his affection. "My only sin," he tells himself, "lies in the fact that I have failed to retain what once I seem to have inspired." In saying this (and nearly all jealous people do say this, or something like it) he is not so far from the truth as might be imagined. At the root of jealousy there is a want of confidence: confidence, obviously, in the other, but a want of confidence also in self. Since there is a wrong and a right kind of self-confidence, it is as well that we should recognise the fruits by their tree. If we trusted each other more and mistrusted ourselves less — in other words, forgot about ourselves — there would be no room for jealousy. So soon as jealousy, with its twofold doubt, enters in, there is at once a loss of balance, a false sense of values and proportion, and though there may not be actual discord in the outward relationship between two individuals of whom one is jealous and the other is on the defence, there can be certainly nothing easy or spontaneous or mellow about their meetings. Tension is felt on both sides: the person who is jealous either playing the pathetic or forcing the pace; the one who isn't jealous but who is having to suffer the effects of it trying to keep up the pretence that everything is perfectly natural. Each is on guard; there is no understanding between them.

Where jealousy is responsible for the breaking up of a relationship, it is nearly always the one who is jealous, and not the other, who takes the initiative and finally cuts adrift. To him it may appear as the great renunciation, but in actual fact it is the result of not being prepared to make the act of faith which love demands. It is want of generosity; there has not been enough trust. He has wanted to get from his love, and not to give to it. "Marriage," says Joyard, "is the kind of game in which the loser always wins." This is true of all human relationships: the exacting are doomed to disappointment. Because disappointed, they give up. "It's hopeless going on with this any more: I had better back out altogether." The dreary finish of what might have been a satisfactory and permanent union is phrased in terms like these.

This brings us to the final examination of our subject. So far we have considered the melancholy effects of jealousy, and though there is hardly an aspect of it that is not melancholy, there is, for the right understanding of its place in the human character, this slight consolation to be considered — that it is a perfectly natural feeling to have. Few people are spared its anxieties in one form or another. With every human love there is the desire to possess, and with this possessiveness there is bound to go an element of jealousy. It is a deviation from the straight, it is an excrescence, it is a slight deformity. Only when the deformity grows, and becomes a limb which absorbs more attention than is given to the rest of the body, does it do any real harm. This, however, need never happen; even those who are constitutionally jealous can take themselves in hand.

If in the will we choose to trust instead of to doubt, if in the will we choose to leave the thing in God's hands and refuse to try and run our love at a personal profit, then what happens in the feelings is of no great consequence. *Of course* in the sensitive appetite there will be affection for creatures, but if our highest energies are reserved for God then neither is the human affection nor the resulting jealousy inordinate. The jealousy is perhaps allowed us as a signal, telling us that our affection will now need watching.

When God is referred to in Scripture as a "jealous" God, we assume at once that He is demanding the repudiation of all human affection. Nowhere does He say so. Is it not much more likely that He is jealous of what we do with our wills? Of the disposition of our affections, provided our choice of Him and His will is not interfered with, God is not jealous. He knows that our sensitive appetites cannot help attaching themselves to creatures. It is their natural function to do so. The only qualification is that they have to be under discipline. The will, united with His, must be in control. We choose God, and give thanks for what He sends. When He Himself has promised to send a hundredfold, it seems unlikely that He is going to be jealous of what we accept from His hands.

To conclude, then, it looks as if jealousy may serve a useful purpose after all: it can let us know when our *amor benevolentiae* is beginning to show signs of becoming *amor concupiscentiae*. It can stimulate our act of confidence; it can remind us of our responsibility, of the need for an asceticism in these things. We must learn to run our relationships without expressed votes of confidence; human affection is cheapened by such declarations. Without a certain austerity of the heart, there is every possibility of jealousy becoming a mania, an obsession which will tend to dry up a soul's interest in God, in people, in life itself. Those who indulge their jealousy become, because their minds work only in the one direction, duller and duller; their punishment is to lose the respect and love of the one person in the world whose opinion of them they care about.

"Where there is jealousy," says St. James, "there you will find disorder and every kind of defect."

All this, and probably a lot more, the young woman in the bus was doubtless thinking as she closed her eyes and mentally listened to the muted strings and soft silken harmonies of her favourite tune.

TRUTH

HE SENSE IN WHICH TRUTH is to be discussed here has nothing directly to do with not telling lies; nor has it to do with being true to a person or to a cause. It is to be thought of simply as meaning conformity. Incidentally all truth is this. Fidelity to causes and people is conformity to the purposed allegiance, just as speaking the truth is conformity with what is believed in the mind of the speaker. An action or course of action which "rings true" is one which conforms to the character of the agent. "It is exactly what you would expect of him": it is a sincere reflexion of what is believed to be his habit of mind. An act or course of action can, accordingly, be true and bad at the same time. A bad man is responsible for truly bad acts; the acts are true to type. A true saint and a true sinner are those whose ways conform, respectively, to the accepted concept of sanctity and sin. Now what this exceedingly boring introduction has been leading up to is this: that the truth of our lives depends on the measure of our conformity with the concept of us that exists in the mind of God. Not with other people's concept of what we are, nor with our own concept of what we would like to be, but simply with the type proposed by God.

Half the battle therefore is to find out what God's concept of us is. The other half is to be true to it. Unfortunately we can mistake God's concept, and so spend a considerable portion of our lives playing a part. In other words being false. Of course this admits of degree: how far we are being bogus we can never quite determine. Self-deception can carry us to alarming lengths, and people will tell you they are being sincerity itself when to everyone else it is patent that they are very wide indeed of their particular mark. Others can see what we cannot always see, and for years we can go on hammering our colours to the wrong mast. To a whole series of masts. The more honest among us do this in the restless search for some sort of truth, the less honest in a vague hope that quantity will compensate for conformity. Perhaps one reason for the confusion which exists in the minds of some, and which prevents them from following their true vocation, is that if God showed them exactly what He wanted of them they would refuse Him. God seems to prefer that His creatures should muddle through in more or less good faith than that they should live for any length of time in thoroughly bad faith. Be that as it may, the fog for which we are responsible is almost always due to our forming images of ourselves which are not the images which God has formed. We are glad enough not to know what our proper image is. We are afraid of picking on the right mast in case it might not show our colours to advantage. It is the colours that we think of first. Then the mast.

The thing is further complicated by reason of the fact that we have to allow for a measure of possible change in our approach to life. Training, environment, and above all God's grace, can bring out all sorts of qualities which nobody would have suspected at the beginning but which have to be considered as the soul advances to maturity. This means that it is not always safe to take advice from people who say: "I have known you since you were so high, and believe me . . ." No, ultimately the responsibility is one's own. One has to find out what God's plan is — regardless of what old friends think it is, regardless of what one would like it to be — and make for that.

"But if I can't look to those who claim to know me, and if I can't be sure of knowing myself, whom can I turn to in my search for a vocation to follow? The saints?" The saints will help, of course, for the general direction, but the saints aren't a book of reference with the litany as an index. Unless we have got the imagination well in control it would be rash to choose out a saint and say: "I'll follow him." We can never be sure that our way is his way. The saint and I are both looking for God's way, but can I be sure that the saint's way and mine lie alongside in the way that leads to God? If there is one drawback to the Church's doctrine of the Communion of Saints it is that we have such a variety of models to choose from. Admittedly it is also the chief advantage. If only we were not liable to single out the romantic element to the exclusion of the real we would not be so easily side-tracked in our choice. After studying the lives of the saints we see ourselves in a variety of possible roles. Who is this gentle kneeling figure? Who is this gruff but kindly apostle? Who is this selfless minister of the sick? Who is this genial and always accessible soul who appears as a man of the world to those who know no better, but who has a secret mystical life tucked away in the background? Who, you ask? You have guessed — it is none other than myself. All of them, they are all me. And I am more besides: I am the confidant of the fallen, the uncomplaining sufferer, the quiet-eyed reader of souls, the one whose singleness of purpose is for ever misconstrued....

Thus is wasted the sanctifying but commonplace service which, only because it has never appeared between inverted commas, has never had the slightest attraction for us. If we are in earnest about the search for our real place in the world and not for a sham platform of our own making, we are more likely to gain light from the cool deliberate practice of a detached self-offering than from any amount of hunting through the guide-books. It is the illustrations of the guide-books which divert us; they show us the beauty spots, so of course we come with the eye of the tourist.

Here is a story about truth. It has not a great deal to do with the above, but it has something to do with it. As such it is worth adding. Besides, it need not be read.

There was once a princess who was so ill at ease among the splendid surroundings of her father's court that she decided to go far away from home and become a simple goose-girl. This she did; and among the geese and on the meadows she found the peace which she had never enjoyed at home. She grew to be loved not only by her flock of rather silly birds, but by animals of every sort, and — so completely did she grow out of the shyness that had weighed upon her in the palace — by her fellow peasants as well. Very soon she forgot the manners of the world, and it was seldom, if ever, that the slightest pang of homesickness pricked her heart. But life, even in a country lane, never stands still for very long, and one evening as she was driving her geese over the brow of a hill before putting them away for the night, she met a prince. She was singing a song of the land at the time, and there was that look in the sky which tells of a very great heat on the morrow. The clouds were high up and evenly spaced, not moving to east or west, and tinged on the under side with the faintest flush of orange. The prince, as it happened, had lost his way while hunting deer, of which there were many in that part. Had the song died on the goose-girl's lips all would have been well, but the goose-girl was singing because she was happy, and it never crossed her mind to stop. Indeed the sight of the prince with the light of the setting sun on his face made her happier still, and she sang more than ever for very joy. This was the first of many meetings. Nothing could have been more seemly than the prince's bearing on every occasion of his visit, while for her part the goose-girl was the perfect blending of ease, of innocence, and of discretion. Each year at the season of hunting the prince would escape from the chase and the two young people would talk about the beautiful, grave, gay, weighty and silly matters which lovers have talked about since the beginning of the world. To the prince's persuasions that she should mix again in the society of the court (for she had told him her story) the goose-girl would always turn a deaf ear. "Geese are my second nature," she would laugh, "and my first wasn't natural at all." Little by little, however, not all at once but little by little, the prince's arguments prevailed, and the goose-girl became more and more drawn away from the peasant life which she had chosen, more and more caught up in the life of the palace. Until finally she accepted the offer to become lady-in-waiting to the queen, the prince's mother. "She was wasted among her geese," said everyone at court, "she was born to our way, and not to that other on the farm." The old shyness which had constrained her long ago in the company of the great and amid the splendours of her father's palace troubled her no more, and the goose-girl was thus led to wonder whether the prince and her new friends had not been right after all in bringing her back to what was originally hers by birth . . . and what was hers now by inclination also. In her heart of hearts she was, nevertheless, uneasy.

Months passed and one day the prince and the goose-girl were walking by the side of a lake in the palace gardens, throwing crumbs at the swans that swam there. "I could no longer go back to my geese," said the goose-girl, "even if I had a mind to do so." This disturbed the prince, but rather than let her see how disturbed he was, and in order to banish such thoughts with their implications from the goose-girl's mind, he doubled his efforts to keep every hour filled for both of them with pleasures and enjoyments of every sort. More months went by, and the goose-girl was found to outdo everyone else at court in the zest with which she pursued the course of amusement which was opened out to her as the result of the prince's perplexed caprice. At last the prince himself, and not the goose-girl, brought the matter to an end. Wishing to regain the days when he had been able to enjoy the company of the goose-girl undisturbed, he prevailed upon his mother to release the goose-girl from her service and to restore her once more to her geese and her meadows and her sunsets and her rough peasant friends who lived all the year round in the folds of their native hills and never saw anybody. The clock was put back, but he was never quite able to recapture the days as they had been before, because, though the goose-girl became a goose-girl again, the spell had been broken and life had gone on. Life could not wait while the two of them made experiments and mistakes, so he went on with being prince and she went on with being a goose-girl. There is only one thing to add, and that is that to the end of his life the prince used, when he thought of the matter at all, which was every now and then, to say: "Well, anyway, she is happier as she is; I am glad I acted unselfishly." What he did not say, for it never crossed his mind to say it, was: "I too am happier as I am; it would have driven me mad to see her wasting on the court the love that was mine for the asking." On second thoughts this story should have come at the end of the foregoing essay and not at the end of this one. Except that if it is our purpose in this book to keep our eyes open, then every essay might fittingly close with a story that explodes a self-deception. If jealousy can pitch its motive so high as to say: "Wouldn't you be more comfortable if I were out of the way? Isn't it trying for you when my jealousy nags at you like this? Hadn't I much better go?" ... then every so-called sacrifice of self upon the altar of another's happiness should be examined and held up to the light of truth. Truth is conformity. We must be sure that our alleged motives conform to our real ones.

PERSONAL INFLUENCE

IT IS A FACT OF COMMON experience that the things which we most admire in our heroes are those which they themselves most value. We do not say: "This is a prince among men: he can do any crossword, however difficult, in less than five minutes." We do not say: "Here is a woman in a thousand; the thought of her will be a beacon to me throughout my life; I like her handwriting." Why do we not say these things? Because there are few people in the world who make it their whole endeavour to pursue the trifling; and still fewer who would notice it if they did.

The attraction, then, is twofold: we are drawn by the conviction, the virtue, the particular doctrine or whatever you like to call it, which is represented by the person whom we admire, and we are drawn by the sincerity with which that person represents it. The implications of this are many.

In the first place, from the point of view of the hero-worshipper and not from that of the hero, it shows up our powers of appreciation. If we admire people for their shallower qualities, then we too must be equally shallow. Our standards are wrong. We estimate trivially. In proportion as we admire good things in others are we potentially good ourselves. *Potentially* good: worth while. The more noble the hero's virtue, the more wise we show ourselves to be in admiring it. The more we admire it, the more are we drawn to imitate it. And so in turn even we become noble. Such is the effect of another's influence.

But it works both ways. Say our hero is a bad man. There is something in us, evidently, that admires the badness in him or he wouldn't be to us a hero. This is distressing. It is nevertheless a practical consideration. When we allow ourselves to be drawn by the unpleasant side of another person, it is not that we are seeing the bad as bad; but that we are forcing ourselves to see it under an appearance of good. It is the show of good which we are following, not the reality of bad. Thus the influence of an evil hero, whether openly bad or simulated good, is in practice equally pernicious. Take a less extreme case. Say our hero has won our admiration on purely trivial grounds: because, for example, he dresses well. Though his influence may not be directly harmful, it is bound to be so negative as to be a waste. His influence over us will be in this particular field of dress; taking our values from the man we admire we shall rate clothes higher than the things which are more important. Our frivolous approach to life will stand exposed: a leader who gives to dress his first attention will not number among his disciples great thinkers, great statesmen, great saints.

Thus it is that cranks normally follow cranks, and that solemn people float sombrely in the wash of people more solemn than themselves. This principle does not cover every case, because for one thing we are often attracted by characteristics which are the opposite of our own, and for another we are capable of fastening upon some quality which is not a significant part of the other person's nature and admiring that. In the main, however, it is true to say that we are attracted by that projection of ourselves in another which we see more forcibly represented there than anywhere else; and that the force of its representation is derived from the importance given to it in the mind of that other person.

Considering now the interaction of character upon character from the point of view of the one who does the influencing rather than the one who is influenced, we see that there is need for great integrity if the effect produced is to have any real value.

To influence others for good a man must, on the showing of the principles just laid down, not only profess to believe in the things that supremely and objectively matter (for there is all the difference in the world between things that matter in their own right and things that matter to us), but he must so value them interiorly that their possession will express itself in his life. The things which you rate highest, whether you speak about them or whether you don't, are those which you will be remembered for when you die. In giving a lead to others it is not enough for a man to preach or write about religion; still less is it enough to hide in himself the evil which is there; he must think positively, must construct, must raise the whole tone of his ideas, must generate a heat of soul. It is a man's idealism, if it is anything, which is going to waken a response. The spark, in order to catch, must be *there*. Something of that fire which Christ came on earth to cast must be glowing all the time, deep down, in the individual; everything else is only propaganda. Do we ever consider that another's course of action — whether now or in ten years' time, whether consciously related to our influence or not — is at the other end of a chain which has started off as something in our mind? Not in our words, primarily, nor in our acts, but in our thoughts. In what else, after all — since it is the inward that determines the outward.

The conclusion is, then, that if I want to rescue from a certain sin either a person or a group of persons (or a country or a generation), I must so practise the corresponding virtue, so value it, so pray it into my life that it works itself finally into the desires of those for whom I labour. The apostles knew no other method.

MORE ABOUT CREATURES

IN THE EPISTLE TO THE Hebrews we read that "it was from things unseen that the things we see took their origin." To the problem of creatures, then, the solution must lie in faith. We are urged, again in Hebrews, to "look forward all the while to that city which has true foundations, which is God's design and God's fashioning." Don't concentrate too much upon what your senses tell you of the thing, but make it your business to go by what you know in faith. The senses go so far and no farther. They are attracted by the superficial, by glamour. When looking at creatures in the face it's hard to keep the unprejudiced eye. Detached, unallured, ordered must be our gaze, not haphazard or hungry or myopic. Faith, the same Epistle tells us, taught Abraham to "live as a stranger in the land he had been promised as his own, encamping there with Isaac and Jacob." In the land which surrounds us, in the created land which is peopled by those we know and mix with and love, we must be careful to encamp and not to take root too deeply. This idea of camping is an inheritance from the Old Testament where the Chosen People were never allowed to settle down for very long without being reminded that they were "no better than strangers and exiles upon earth." St. Paul is constantly emphasising to the descendants of Israel the fact that "they have not found their home." Life for us must be a bivouac business, always more or less on the move. Allow ourselves the luxury of permanent dwellings, and we cease to look out for the land of promise. We are strangers among the things of sense, always slightly homesick for the city not made with hands. So long as we are homesick we are safe: it is when we no longer value our spiritual citizenship that we are in danger. The apostasy takes place when the foreigner assumes that he is a native, when he no longer prides himself on being a misfit. The word "worldling" suggests to us the trappings of the night-club, the racecourse, and the expensive hotel; but anyone can be a worldling. A worldling is simply a person who has made his home among creatures, and who looks for nothing more from life. He may or may not enjoy this kind of existence, he may or may not be able to live down to his tastes, but if he ceases to think of this life as a time spent in tents he is a man of the world, he is of the earth, earthy.

Creatures, in other words, must not be looked to for a content which they were never meant to have. Loved, certainly, but approached with the undazzled eye. The moment we close our fingers round a joy, it escapes us. If we look for a box in which to put our ecstasy, we wake up. Experience teaches us this every day of our lives, yet again and again we catch ourselves trying to crystallise an emotion, an appreciation, a flash. These things are meant to be passing. A point of view which seemed crystal clear to us yesterday may be meaningless today; an intuition which felt as if it was going to provide anchorage for the rest of our lives may have drained itself of interest almost before it had time to bring any practical light to bear; a burning desire is stillborn overnight. Is this very shocking? Not necessarily. It is very natural. We *can't* hold on. We can't put our finger on the screen as the film flicks across it, and say: "Stop, I like this bit . . . I want it to stay like this for ever." The whole point of a movie is that it moves. The show goes on. Life is like that: no waiting. If, moreover, we try and force it — try and seal up our happiness and keep it from evaporating — not only does it, as has already been suggested, turn sour on us, but it also has the effect of spoiling our taste for the other and more lasting happiness. Nothing atrophies so inevitably, when blunted by spurious satisfactions, as the faculty of appreciation. The time comes when we don't know happiness when we see it. We can't think of happiness apart from excitement, and if this excitement is absent we judge the happiness to be a very tame affair. "Give us our luxuries and we won't ask for our necessities." It is so easy to accept the second best, and substitute amusement for genuine joy. Amusement, provided always that it can be kept up, has the enormous advantage which not even work (or the spiritual life) can claim: it can so absorb the waking hours that there is nothing left over for anything else. "Wars and years roll by"—I quote from a letter—"but we're still dancing at the Mayfair." Dare any of us say that we can always tell the true from the false—let alone choose it when we do know? We who can so easily mistake prettiness for beauty are quite as maddeningly ready to mistake entertainment for happiness. For one thing we don't have to look so far or wait so long: it's pleasant to get things by return of post. We ask for an egg, but are quite ready to accept, on immediate delivery, a good-looking scorpion.

There was once a young man, a poet, who decided to go in search of beauty and happiness. (It was foolish of him to bracket the two together like this because one is in the things you look at and the other is in the way you look at them; but the young man was so sure that he had only to find beauty to find happiness as well that he made the youthful mistake of lumping the two together and hoping for the best.) Quite early in his travels the young man came to a meadow where there was a butterfly resting upon a leaf. But when he put out his finger to stroke the butterfly, the wings crumbled away immediately to dust. So he went further and came to an orchard where he saw the pink of apple-blossom gleaming clear against the blue sky. But when he plucked a sprig of it the petals came apart and fluttered to the ground at his feet. "Evidently," said the poet to himself, "the thing is not to touch beauty, or I shall find that I can't keep happiness. Next time

I must be content to stand by and watch." After this he walked for many miles until he reached a cottage where there was a young girl sitting framed in a doorway. The sun was playing in the girl's hair and there was the soft humming of bees. "I will stay here looking at this for ever," said the young man, "and I shall be happy." But though the sun came every day to light up the girl's hair, and though the bees continued to hum, and though the young man kept to his resolve about standing aside and not being greedy, there was still something missing. As the girl grew older the hair began to lose its lustre, and eventually the bees who had been so faithful with their humming swarmed elsewhere, and the young man was obliged to set off once more upon his journey. "Everything fades sooner or later," he said to himself; "nothing remains the same ... there is no lasting loveliness even in youth." It was with a heavy heart that he pursued his quest, but he had not despaired. At last one evening at the turn of summer when the sky was grey but not with rain, and when the warmth of day still glowed in the grass and in the whitewashed walls of farms and peasant houses, he came to a place where an old woman was washing clothes by a stream. The old woman's fingers, beneath the foam of soap, were like the roots of an ancient vine, and on her feet were great boots like a soldier's. Something must have saddened her for she was crying softly to herself as she bent over the wet things. "There is beauty in old age," confessed the young man, "and there is beauty in sorrow." But even as he spoke, the tear dried on the old woman's cheek, and she shuffled off heavily to her supper. "It is no use," he said, "I had better give up." But he went on all the same. Finally he came many years later to the shores of a great sea. It was night and the time of full moon, and the light danced silver green on the surface of the water. "I will not stay here," said the poet, "for sooner or later a cloud will pass before the face of the moon, and I shall be where I was before." As he turned to go, being still ready to continue his search, he found that he was in the presence of an angel. "You are right," said the angel. "But perhaps," he added, "you will find what you want in this." So saying, he handed to the young man a piece of bread. "It isn't even beautiful," said the young man rather sadly. "No, but it is nourishing," replied the angel, "and you can't have everything." The young man took the bread that was offered him, but by the time he had raised it to his lips the bread had turned to stone. After this he did not look for happiness any more.

It doesn't do to make the pursuit of happiness our main concern. There is the danger that we may not know it when we've got it. We can't help wanting it, but as to our having it, that is God's affair. For us to get on with the business of living. Happiness is a by-product.

LEADERSHIP

HE ABOVE TITLE SENDS SHIVers down the spine, but there seems to be no other word. The dictionary suggests captaincy, but this too is a word we could do without. Even when we get round it by talking of the quality that inspires, or the instinct to command, or the assumption of control, we are not on happy ground. Leadership it will have to be.

What is it that the leader has and others have not? Magnetism? Charm? Compelling personality? Certainly these three come in, but leadership would seem to be something more — some undefined characteristic of mind that holds the reins and gives these lesser natural advantages their head when need requires. When we think of the leader we think of the firm blue eye and the tiller held in the steady hand. Mentally we rank ourselves among the led. The thing is too big for us. We can be hero-worshippers, yes, but not heroes. The dismal part about it is that the older we get the less we tend to be hero-worshippers, let alone heroes. But there is the germ of leadership in everyone. Not for all the showy kind with the banner and the head raised high, but for all the vocation to influence others. The disciples may be few, the influence may be so subtle as to go almost unrecognised, the reward may escape this life altogether, but certain it is that God gives to every soul the chance of being an apostle. To each of us is measured an ability for handling souls, even if it is to handle no more than one. I know of two men whose work is parallel and whose influence is considerable: with one the appeal and effect are spread out, with the other concentrated. It is difficult to say which does the more good: the one with the wider circle or the one who makes the deeper impression. Not that it matters, because neither is envious of the other, or is in any way trying to run a stud. The point is that each is working his talent, each is being true to himself, each is developing his own technique. With most of us the temptation is to bury the talent, to overlay the true self, to borrow someone else's technique. This is laziness. It sometimes calls itself humility, but it is sheer unwillingness to bother. We are shy of using the gifts we've got, and we excuse ourselves on the grounds that other people have been given much greater ones. This is no excuse at all. We see leadership in another man's face, we hear it in what he says, we feel it in the electricity of his presence, we read it in his letters, and we say: "I can't compete with this." We aren't *meant* to. All we are asked to do is to live our own life, and live it to the full. Live, not vie with. Life itself is a talent. Vitality is almost the whole stuff of leadership. The generation of energy is precisely its magnetism. It is the same whether you are considering the physical or intellectual or spiritual order. Hero, genius, saint: the motor force in each is life. We have at least that one talent in common with the experts, and if our lives radiate outwards instead of remaining folded up within, it is inconceivable that there should be none to take our proffered lead. No spectacular leadership is this, no assumption of rights or expressed recognition, but simply the relationship which results from the outgoing of a soul. In the very dedication of self to the service of others, even if the others are unspecified and not yet on the horizon, there is an appeal which must inevitably be answered. It is an appeal which we have a right to make. To exercise an appeal is not at all the same as to allure; to exploit allure in the search for a following would be fatal. Appeal here is no more than the sheen of generosity; allure is, at best, carefully directed glamour.

Laziness and false humility are not the only reasons why people are slow to encourage a responsive group of disciples. There is also the fear of evoking hostility. You know that the moment your circle begins to form itself criticisms will be multiplied. Let them be. A typical instance is: "Among those whom these zealous souls collect round them are noticeably the interesting and exciting; it would be more impressive if the flock consisted of bores and cranks." A cruel thrust, but of course the answer is that the interesting and exciting people need far more looking after than any others.

It is because they are interesting and exciting that they will be tempted; the dull and irritating are to be helped and sympathised with, but certainly their trying qualities make them far less vulnerable. All who need care of any sort are to be received and even sought out, but to imagine that the attractive personalities are to be given second place on the grounds that it is more meritorious to labour for the boring than the charming is a complete misconception. It shouldn't be a question of which work is the more meritorious but which is the more necessary. Which does the more good? — not to me but to the world at large?

It is in the nature of the critic to see in another's work the rewarding aspect, and not at all the disappointing. Or he sees the success, and fails to notice the effort that has gone to make the success. All the more is this the case — and it is a pardonable mistake to make — when the whole fruit of a man's work is dependent upon the apparent carelessness of its execution. The easy and ample manner of those who are sometimes the best apostles is deceptive: if they showed more of the rough working that has been going on in the margin they would be less criticised by the envious. But to have revealed the technique would have spoiled the work; it would have cramped their style; they would have become stilted and self-conscious. People who lead others over difficult country adopt a pace and manner that is unhurried and unprofessional; the more difficult the country the more effortless must the guidance appear. This is both easier to keep up with and easier to imitate. But you won't get the people who are marching stiffly on the parade-ground to understand this. What the world at large doesn't realise is that leadership isn't just whistling for admirers and then sitting back to enjoy adulation. The disappointments, to take only one thing, are greater to the man who has the care of others than to those who have none but themselves to worry about. Who, however limited his influence, has not experienced that liquefaction of hope and heart which comes with the news of another's failure? It is as if something had collapsed inside and one's whole being was running away to waste. That a person of whom we had expected everything should go back on a lead we have given him is an experience so bitter that the memory of it remains with us all our lives. This happens once or twice to us who have perhaps little influence on the world in which we live. It must happen often to the leader. Nor is it the kind of agony which diminishes with repetition. Add to these disappointments the constant fears and anxieties of not knowing how far the loyalty can be stretched, how clearly the terms of sacrifice are understood, how deeply the whole thing has sunk in, how long the influence will last.... The leader, no less than the led, has need of great faith, great trust, great love.

As there are trials for those who are called by God to help others, so are there pitfalls. They can become exacting, overbearing, pompous, petty, hard. They can become childishly vain, mistaking flatterers for followers; they can prostitute their gift and wallow in the power it gives them instead of using it for those whom they are meant to help. To rejoice in leadership and neglect to lead is surely the last degradation. So common is this that it is not recognised for the travesty that it is. Guidance (a bad word, scented by association with the Oxford Group, and used here only in order to ring the changes on the other bad, but less bad, word "leadership") can become a hobby, can become even an obsession. Guidance can captivate the mind to the exclusion of sympathy. You have the director pouring oil on troubled waters for the sake of pouring oil, and not for the sake of the troubled waters. All work for others is in danger of becoming an end in itself: stopping short at a level of selfishness and not going on to the unmeasured giving which knows no level of any sort. The writer, the preacher, the reformer, the priest — each can forget his public, and think only of his publicity.

To meet the drawbacks, the snares, the temptations, the criticisms attendant upon the exercise of leadership there can be in the end, then, only one answer: love. Compelled thereto by love, the leader need have no fear of his power, nor of his following, nor of his responsibility. "And I if I be lifted up will draw all things": here is his text, here his model Leader. Draw, not push; lead, not propel. Draw, too, towards Christ and not towards self. But it will mean being lifted up, it involves the Cross. But love can bear it, just as love can bear all else. Charity is not only the end, it is also the means. Without charity the leader is nothing but a thruster: a man can push his way to the fore, and he can drag others after him, but if he lacks sympathy he lacks leadership. Without charity—so far as working as a Christian goes—there is no point in giving a lead; without charity there is no point in being led. "Love like mine," wrote Browning, "must have return." Applied to loving humanity, the words take on a new direction. Return is given to a leadership which has charity; nothing but resentful obedience can be given to a leadership which has not. No quality communicates itself more effectively than love; even hate can't put up more barriers than charity pulls down.

TAKING THE SMOOTH WITH THE ROUGH

TO THE ORDINARY UNTRAINED mind, the bee is the symbol of industry. We judge the bee as having a single, and even rather gross, purpose. "Nothing but honey, honey, honey —morning, noon and night." Then on investigation we learn that honey interests the bee hardly at all. The bee's main preoccupation is, apparently, building.[*] Whether this is the case or not, it illustrates a principle which is exceedingly important in the affairs of human beings. Provided the appropriate purpose of the individual is served, the byproduct may take what shape it likes. Often the by-product has (as in the case of the honey coming over and above the work of building) more publicity-value than the labour which produces it. This in itself doesn't matter in the least. It is only when the by-product is rated higher than the natural product that there is likely to be trouble. It is when the bee says: "why bother about building when we've got a gold mine in this honey business?" that the betrayal of purpose begins. Not only does building become a bore to the bee (which it never was before), but honey becomes a bore as well (which again it never

---

[*] As is also, one is told, the ant's.

was before). Our first duty is to answer the requirements of our particular vocation; once we are working away faithfully at that, we have every reason to look forward to the honey. Happiness, like honey, comes as an extra. Life itself, with its job and its cross and its weary responsibilities, comes first. If we are greedy for the honey we become so anxious about it that we haven't room to enjoy it.

There is too much talk about man being made for happiness, and not enough about what he's to do with it when he's got it. To concentrate on the satisfaction which is designed to meet man's natural craving leads only to an increase of the craving and a lessening of the satisfaction. Though man may be destined for happiness, the act of craving for it is not a happy act. There are some who seem to be so hungry for happiness that they are never ready to acknowledge that they've got it. They look for satisfaction everywhere and are disappointed when they are uncomfortable. Life seems to them rough because they are always expecting it to be smooth. But who ever said that life was meant to be smooth? The only way is to take the rough and give thanks for the smooth. Christ's burden is light and sweet only when it has been accepted as a burden. There is an order to be observed in these things, and if the order is reversed the object is missed.

It is a mistake to look upon happiness as something which is granted to man over and above his ordinary life, as a sort of prize for good conduct or as a compensation for rough treatment. A by-product emerges from the work of production; it is not superimposed from without. Happiness is not something which we feel we have a right to in our free time; it emerges from the set-up of our lives; it is the colour of our work; it has nothing to do with being in or out of office hours; it must not be confused with recreation. As always it is a question of getting back to the sermon on the mount which is the clearest statement of principle that the world has ever listened to. "Seek ye first the kingdom of God and all these things shall be added to you." Happiness comes naturally if you let it. Look for it you must, but don't look for it anxiously or with one eye upon the happiness of others. Take it, together with unhappiness, in your stride. Ungrudging with regard to others, ungreedy with regard to yourself.

To a large extent our experience of happiness is conditioned by our view of unhappiness. Or, more precisely, by our view of suffering. If we look upon suffering as a purely fortuitous happening to be avoided by every possible means, we shall look upon happiness as an escape. But suffering is something more significant than a chance circumstance. Happiness is something more than an escape. Suffering, like happiness, is part of life itself, and to come to the end of one's life having more or less by-passed suffering is to have lived incompletely. Suffering, like happiness, is to be taken in one's stride. Like happiness again, but for very different reasons, it doesn't do to concentrate on it.

Some people think that though sorrows are natural enough in anyone's life, unhappiness is wrong—a vice. But surely there are people who have never decided to indulge their sorrow, who have never broadcast their woes, who have never embarked deliberately upon anything so obviously stultifying as self-pity, yet who at the same time are quite definitely not happy. Unhappiness to them is a malformation: inseparable and not culpable. But because even deformities can be exploited for selfish ends, a settled unhappiness must never be allowed free rein. It is a weak and miserable specimen who hides behind his wretchedness, and looks over the barrier only to invite Sympathy. "Sorrow doth not spring out of the ground," says the holy man Job. It comes, like joy, from God. And, like joy, it must be referred back again to God. Only so can it be prevented from becoming selfishness or waste. But don't think that by giving it back to God you can get rid of it. You can't. Sorrows, and even periods of acute unhappiness, are inevitable to the make-up of man; but sorrow, and even unhappiness, can well be squared with the settled serenity of the soul whose anchorage is God.

BITTERNESS

I WAS ONCE AS A SMALL BOY a spectator of a fight, in Alexandria, between a Greek barber and an Arab newspaper seller. It happened like this. The Greek, who was clearly the aggressor throughout, dashed from his shop and slashed the Arab's face with a razor. The traffic stopped, the crowd took sides, advice was shouted in five languages, and the little girl who was with me in the carriage was sick over the cushions. To add to the excitement of the scene (which to the fastidious might seem to be already overcharged), the lady about whom the battle was being fought leaned out from an upper window and proclaimed, through her tears, that if the combatants did not at once desist she would hurl herself into the street. Such was the picture. Now in spite of so many promising circumstances, I knew, even at the age of six, that there was not here the material for a fight of the highest quality: the weapon used was not the traditional cut-throat but the ordinary Gillette blade held between thumb and forefinger. (This was long before the gangster movement had popularised the single edged "carver," which can be so held that it does no harm to the man who is using it.)

Bitterness, like a Gillette blade unskilfully handled in the to-and-fro of a razor fight, can do a certain amount of harm to other people, but it can very often do far more harm to oneself. A bitter man may be destructive in what he says, may cause mischief, may dash the hopes of those who are ready to start off with a flourish of trumpets, *but he is the sufferer in the long run*. Bitterness is the extension of a bad mood; it jabs continuously at other people, and all the time the blade goes deeper and deeper into oneself.

It is a curious and fatal tendency on the part of human beings that they tend to work up a grievance against people whom they have treated unjustly. Discovered in a critical judgment we dig ourselves in when we should be digging ourselves out. Not only can we be unfair in this way to people, but we can be unfair in exactly the same way with principles. We can be bitter towards ideals, towards certain aspects of religion, towards authority in general, and very, very often towards the circumstances of our life. God gives us life and we bear a grudge against it. God gives us the Gospel and we resent its implications. God surrounds us with His representatives and we cling to grievances about them. "I brought thee out of Egypt, and thou hast delivered me to the chief priests . . . I opened the sea before thee, and thou hast opened my side . . . I gave thee the water of salvation to drink, and thou hast given me gall and vinegar . . . I gave thee a royal sceptre, and thou hast given me a crown of thorns . . . I have exalted thee with power, and thou hast hanged me on a gibbet." That is exactly what we do: we go on from ingratitude to malice. And that is bitterness.

The mere desire to hurt someone else is a hurt done to ourselves. It lowers the whole thing; it makes us animal. It is not the part of Christ-redeemed man to bare the teeth and snarl. The most dangerous snarling is the secret kind: the venomous kind which at first sight is dripping with honey. Cruelty, as we know from the scene in Gethsemani, can begin with a caress. The poor jaundiced soul who has made a condition for itself of bitterness is seldom brazen about it; it knows that to grumble is to bore. With the result that the poison is spread with subtlety, sprayed fine over unsuspecting soil. That is the awful part. You find you have assimilated the cynic's habit of mind before you have fully recognised him as a cynic. There may be pain and trouble and even a certain amount of rebellion in doing the will of God, but there should certainly not be bitterness. Cynicism cannot come from God. It is in the highest interests of the devil to persuade the world that religious people are disagreeable. A great many undoubtedly are, but it is not in virtue of their religion; it is in virtue of their lack of it. Joy comes from God, and the devil knows this so well that if he can show himself capable of providing a joy of his own which will discredit the joy of God's service, his battle is virtually won. For those then who profess to serve God — or at all events for those who are trying to — it is vitally necessary that they profess geniality as well.

The Greek hairdresser was led away screaming with rage and mortification. The Gillette blade was taken away from him, and his hand was bandaged up with one of the towels out of his own shop. What happened to the Arab and the lady upstairs I never knew. Had the incident taken place today the weapon would presumably have been an electric razor, and the assailant would have had to hit his victim over the head with it at the end of a flex. We can see in this the march of civilisation.

INTEGRITY

INTEGRITY IS, IN ITS PERFECtion, a very rare virtue. Strictly speaking it is a quality which does not admit of degrees: you have got it or you haven't—like a taste for modern art. The word "integrity" comes from the Latin and means "whole"—nothing left out, no mental reservations, nothing up the sleeve—and in this sense is not a relative but an absolute attribute. Yet we know people who have more of it than others; we talk of people being "more or less straight" when what we mean is that they are crooked. Integrity has come to mean "straightness." It is a virtue which is unmistakable: the sincere man, the person who is forthright and open in his dealings with others, stands out at once. Among double- and treble- and quadruple-faced people the single-faced character is a tonic. He is called (by those who do not shrink from the term) a white man. White, presumably, because he is candid. Candour at once suggests bluntness, but this is not what it really means; it means not being grey, not being mixed. "Give me your candid opinion" is very often an invitation to be as brutal as you like; it should, however, be an invitation to speak the truth—to avoid duplicity. There are very few who are not guilty of duplicity in one form or another. It isn't that most of us consciously lead double lives; it is rather that nearly all have got a fold in their characters somewhere. We are "duplex," folded over, covered up. Whether from fear of being disliked by others or of being exposed even to ourselves, we hide. Always a little disguised, always behind a barricade.

People will tell you that it is hypocrisy to behave pleasantly towards those for whom one feels a violent dislike. But *is* it false to exploit what little there is of good in one's nature, and to stifle what much there is of bad? If it is humbug to show a pleasant manner towards those for whom you have an unpleasant regard, it is scarcely less humbug to go two miles gladly with those who invite you to go with them one. You have to rule out your inclinations and simply do the generous thing. Being true means acting up to the best that you are capable of, not the worst. Conformity with the picture God has of you, not with the devil's. The fact that you probably approach nearer to the unpleasant picture than to the pleasant one is no reason why you should strengthen the likeness by acting down to it. Hypocrisy comes in only where there is an attempt to paint a picture of your own — a flattering version bearing no relation to the real you. Here is something positive; here is deception. It is only people who possess the virtue of integrity to a high degree that can be faithful in self-portraiture. And they are precisely the people who don't want to. Humility is a part of their completeness. So also is charity a part of their completeness. Which is why they can say kind things of those who make them feel unkind. To say that conformity with the real is more important than conformity with the ideal is a hopeless doctrine. Man is a rational animal, and to allow him the free exercise of his animal nature on the plea that it feels more real to him at times than his rational nature would be absurd. If a man behaves like a beast, for heaven's sake don't let him say that he's being sincere about it. He is as much a hypocrite as the man who parades a holiness which he hasn't got. More so. He has been made in the image and likeness of God. If he pretends that he has been made in the image and likeness of beasts he is a hypocrite upside down.

So complicated can the thing become that people will think themselves hypocrites if they don't admit that they are hypocrites — which shows that the only thing to do is to make for the model man, Christ, and think as little of oneself as possible. Indeed the "whole" man, the integrated man, *is* only whole and integrated in the measure that he is, as St. Paul says, "formed again in Christ." We can only be ourselves to the full when — such is the paradox — we are being *alteri Christi*. It is only when we have surrendered our personalities to His personality that we find we have any real personality of our own.

SEX

EVELYN WAUGH MAKES A CHARacter in one of his books deplore the fact that as a subject sex has been played to a standstill; it can no longer be used, complains this saddened publicist, for purposes of shocking the average man. Most people would probably agree, however, that in the uphill struggle against competition, sex still manages to hold its own fairly well.

The really shocking aspect of the subject is not so much the nature of the publicity given to it — though this is bad enough — as the complete absence of conscience which is revealed whenever sex is mentioned. The drift is not against morality, but apart from it: amoral rather than immoral. People take it for granted that there is no moral standard from which to depart. It is assumed that there is neither virtue nor vice in sex. As a purely biological fact it is, from the point of view of experience, either rather fun or rather a bore. The moral issue is sidestepped. So Evelyn Waugh's fictitious cynic is likely soon to be proved right; the sensation value of sex is on the decline, and something else will have to be found to take its place. The day is coming when sex will not be news.

It is the consequences of this drift which are so shocking. Shocking, for instance, that modesty is not valued any more. Shocking, too, that unchastity is not only allowed for but taken to be the normal thing. At one time the virtues and vices connected with sex were recognised, even in England, *as* virtues and vices; now they are regarded as eccentricities or quaint fancies. In every class the virtues were taught, were insisted upon, were romanticised. In every class, too, the vices were censured, and it was looked upon as a duty to correct the vicious. People felt sorry when they heard of moral failures, and the people who had themselves failed felt very sorry indeed. Very little of this now. The pure are looked upon as being prudes; the impure as being unwise. No more than that—unwise.

The Christian idea of sex, with its ideals and its safeguards, is no longer understood. It is not even *known*. Perhaps this twofold deficiency is to be traced to our fathers who approached the subject of sex instruction too much on tiptoe, but surely just as much to blame is the non-Christian character of the influences to which everyone is now subject. What the ordinary child used to get by the mere fact of his growing up in a Christian family is today countered by what he gets from the cinema, the novel, the divorce-court news. For the modern boy or girl the home life is very often not *there*. Even if there is a life going on at home, it is often not of a kind from which much good can be learned. As a substitute you have the school. Instruction given at school is bound to be a less natural and spontaneous business, and often it is delivered in such a vague way that only the very intelligent are able to make anything of it. In many schools you get boys and girls primed up with facts and warnings, but left without sufficient principles with which either to relate the facts to life or to see the warnings in perspective.

Whatever the causes of ignorance in this generation regarding sex matters, it is not for want of information about certain aspects of it. The quantity of knowledge (though not the quality) which resounds brassily from the sound-screen assures us that an iron curtain policy is no longer being pursued. Future students of psychology and history will have to judge between the relative demerits of too great silence and too great frankness. The old evil used to be: "I don't believe in telling my boy about all that . . . only puts ideas into his head . . . time enough when he gets married." The result of this was that knowledge came with a shock; and came moreover with experience, which is not the way that it is meant to come. The evil today is: "I don't believe in telling my boy all that . . . sees it wherever he goes . . . he can pick it up that way." The result is that he picks it up wrong. An ignorance of actualities is less harmful than an ignorance of the laws which are designed to govern them when the actualities come to light. The world today sees and hears sex to a nauseating degree, but it hasn't the faintest idea what it's all for.

"Well, what is it for?" might here be objected. "My worldly friends tell me it's for pleasure; my more serious-minded friends tell me it's for keeping up the birth rate; I suppose you're going to tell me it's for God."

"Yes," I would answer, "ultimately for God." The natural order (I would go on to explain) is a thing in itself good. Good for man; good all round. When referred to the glory of God, the natural order is being exercised according to its truest and highest function. It was for this purpose that God created it. Bringing God into the natural order, even into the things of sense and appetite, is therefore not an introduction; it is merely allowing the proprietor his rights. It is not an act of devotion to be performed by those who happen to be religiously minded; it is the obvious thing to do. The natural order leads on directly to the supernatural order. If to relate the two in this way is not so obvious to us now as it might be, this is because of original sin. We have lost the power of seeing life as a whole. Before the Fall things would have been different: we should have had no difficulty in fitting things like sex into the picture. In fact the picture would have been incomplete without it. We would have taken for granted that sex was part of our general make-up. In the Garden of Eden there would have been nothing nasty in the thought of sex. There is now. Sin has drawn a film over the innocent eye of man. We can't, now, look at sex as we would look at a sunset; we can't listen to it as we would listen to the sound of the sea. There are "sexual" associations. But for all that, the natural order is still the natural order. It is a good thing. For us the only need is consciously and deliberately to allow the supernatural order to govern it.

The editor of a popular daily paper once wrote to me asking for an article under the heading *Is Sex O. K.?* I sent him a somewhat formidable statement of the Catholic view, the burden of my remarks being "As things are, no *sir*"; but it was evidently thought that the doctrine of original sin had rather spoiled the fun, and that consequently the public would not be interested, because I heard no more about it. I am not even sure that the manuscript was returned. It was a very dull article.

We make a mistake, then, if we think that sex is something essentially evil. It isn't. It's good; but it's not as safe as it was, that's all. The Stoic philosophers said that the only good was virtue, the only evil was vice. Whatever was not either virtuous or vicious was indifferent. Not more or less indifferent, but really indifferent. On a level were poverty, wisdom, pain, ignorance, friendship, beauty, sex, and so on. The modern pagan holds a philosophy something after this sort, but though in theory he may see nothing moral or immoral about the "indifferents," his experience of them will tell him, if he is honest with himself, that the Christian view is the right one. He will admit with us that there is nothing *really* indifferent. Either the direction, or the motive, or the circumstances, or the hundred and one cross currents which qualify the character of the so-called indifferent ingredients to life must make them either good or bad. Not necessarily giving to them an absolute goodness or an absolute badness — this would never be claimed on the strictest view — but at least making them relatively better or worse. Things like loneliness, health, riches, pleasure and so on can't always and in everybody's experience be altogether neutral. In other words there is nothing so indifferent that man cannot make it either sanctifying or the reverse. Sex can be used as the highest expression of praise. God has intended that He should be praised by it. Sex can also be used for the degrading of man and the offending of God.

Obviously if we form our ideas of beauty, love, human happiness upon the principles advocated by those back-to-nature magazines which are so generously displayed upon our bookstalls we shall miss the whole point. (Equally poisonous is the influence of that other class of body-line literature which boasts of being good clean dirt and no culture: beauty doesn't come in here at all except as prettiness, and love is vulgarised far beyond the flirtation level.) It makes one sick with misery and apprehension to see young people lapping up the wrong sort of stuff simply because they have never had the right sort of stuff put before them. Given an ideal, given the solid truth, they respond at once. They *know* it's worth while, and that the other isn't. I remember instructing a boy under my care on what are called, unrevealingly, the facts of life. At the end of it he said this: "Good heavens, so *that's* the answer. Well, I do call that beautiful, don't you? Really beautiful. And to think that until this moment I simply hadn't a clue."

It *is* beautiful. All that people are waiting for is the clue.

INTERIOR PRAYER: ITS EXPRESSION

CARDINAL GASQUET ONCE preached a course of sermons in America on the subject of prayer and its various stages and states. When the last of these sermons had been delivered, the Cardinal received from a parish priest the following tribute. "Eminence," said the priest, "in spite of what they say about our American advertising methods, you English have got us cold when it comes to putting over a rare commodity like prayer. If you had just said the whole process was as simple as pie nobody would have listened to you more than ten minutes. But the way you split it up and labelled it and tucked it away and brought it out again and measured it and finally gave the impression that no one could be sure of getting it right anyway was really swell. You've certainly got these congregations mad keen to try. I call that mighty subtle, because as you and I know, Eminence"—and here a conspiratorial look crept into the speaker's eye—"it's the easiest thing out." The Cardinal used to tell this story with gusto for it delighted him very much. "One envies the good father his facility," he would say, "and it shows how idle can be these divisions and categories when it comes to praying and not merely talking about prayer."

Certainly to sort out your prayer in the endeavour to get it tidy is a mistake; its neatness can become the main preoccupation and so a distraction. On the other hand it would also be a mistake, surely, to envy a soul's ability to pray with the ease which was evidently experienced by the Cardinal's visitor. Prayer is meant to be simple but not easy. The higher the soul mounts in prayer the simpler it becomes, but also the harder. If you find it as easy as pie to begin with, give thanks to God for it but don't expect it to go on like that for ever. God is drawing you by consolation to practise what you would perhaps not practise without. When He is sure of your generosity He will remove the sense of satisfaction and invite you to go on praying with no other incentive but that of pleasing Him. Always the soul must be reminded that we pray because we love God and not because we love prayer. If love of prayer is our motive, then our service of God is a culture and not a religion. A culture may express itself as elaborately as it likes, but love tends to express itself simply. We may use many forms and formulae when we start off upon our course of prayer, but if we persevere and make of it a life, and not merely a series of exercises, we shall find that in the end our activity reduces itself to something very simple. Love has little use for multiplicity; love is direct and obvious and is not bothered about originality. Love has no interest in method, in polished phrase, in finding new modes of expression. The ordinary language of one word is quite enough. Love songs and love letters are all very much the same; and though each singer and writer knows that his experience is unique, he isn't worried at not being able to produce for his beloved something that has never been produced before. Love is not ashamed to repeat itself. Love thrives on banal repetition. The blessed in heaven are engaged in saying nothing more than "*Sanctus . . . Sanctus . . . sanctus.*" Simple. But to our finite minds which look for something to catch hold of, not easy. Not easy to understand how the angels in heaven and the people who pray on earth can, in the exercise of such a simple prayer, have enough to think about. We imagine that in order to pray properly we have to proceed from one thought to another. We forget that absorption can take the place of all this; we do not have to probe and tabulate and refer back. There is not much speculation, and scarcely anything that is reflex, about the love of God. The search is not tense, there is no anxious straining of the soul; the longing is sometimes painful, but never nervous or excited. The love of God differs from the love of creatures at least in this, that serenity has the final word. The soul that cannot allow itself to relax in prayer must look once again to the nature and purpose of the whole thing. It must face itself honestly and ask, "Am I praying for what I can give or for what I can get?" If my prayer is a busy, fussy, worried time, a time which makes me feel I am under observation and which leaves me on edge, then there is reason to believe that I have got the emphasis wrong, and that there is more of self in it than of God. The freedom of the child in its father's house is our model. Very different is this from the self-consciousness of the caller.

INTERIOR PRAYER: ITS MATERIAL

"WHAT YOU HAVE JUST BEEN saying," the reader objects as he turns the page, "may quite well apply to those whose prayer is a language of love. I know it *should* be this, but all I can say is that for ordinary people like me it's nothing of the sort. It's no use talking to me about being absorbed in the love of God when it's as much as I can do not to get up and walk out. You tell me not to bother about handing illuminated addresses to the Almighty in my prayer, but if I try simplifying the process the whole thing becomes a blank and I don't say any prayers at all. I don't mind in the least about not being fluent or original but I do like to know that there's something going on."

Let us get back to the beginning. God and the soul. Prayer the link between. Because God comes first in the relationship, the nature of the intercourse must be more His than the soul's. Spiritual, in other words, not material. We are not pure spirits like the angels, but soul and body. Flesh and blood perceive flesh and blood. We can't, as we are, perceive God. We can only grope towards Him through what we do perceive. That is why the things of sense are there — so that we may perceive, by faith, God. In relating ourselves to God by prayer we work upwards, through material things to spiritual things. Though there may be much that is material in it, the correspondence between the soul and God is essentially spiritual. It can't, since God is pure spirit, be anything else. Now turn to the concrete case of the human soul working its way up to God, through material things, in prayer.

At the beginning there is what writers call sensible devotion: fervour roused in the senses and by the senses. Objects of piety stir the soul to prayer. Relics, ceremonies, pictures, the sacramentals are found to be an enormous help to prayer. That is what they are for. The material element here is obvious. From these helps that can be seen or performed, the soul goes one higher and makes use of helps that operate more interiorly: it meditates while doing the Stations of the Cross or while saying the rosary. The material element is still there, but the spiritual is beginning to take its place. The images which are formed in the mind are suggested by outward physical things, but it is the mind that is doing the work. It is the beginning of mental prayer. Imagination is painting the pictures, memory is framing them and hanging them up. But there is still too much of sense in this for the requirements of really interior prayer, so the soul goes on to the next stage where there is hardly anything of sense at all. This is where the intellect and will come into their own. This is spiritual prayer. This is the proper correspondence between the soul and God.

"It all sounds very high to me," is what you are saying. It isn't. It's the normal development, under the influence of grace, of most souls who give themselves to prayer. There is nothing mystical about it; it is simply the way that grace and nature combine to produce a perfectly ordinary, though spiritual, effect. This is not to say that the gift of interior prayer inevitably results, or that the soul mechanically mounts the scale of faculties such as we have described; it is merely claimed here that fidelity to the practice of prayer normally leads to the state in which the appropriate activity is not one of sense or imagination or discourse or speculation, but is ordinarily one of the will. It is therefore more subtle and more simple. It is also more sanctifying. In proportion as the act of prayer approaches the act of faith the more salutary it must be to the soul, as well as the more pleasing to God. And the whole point about this prayer that is being weaned away from the senses is that it is nearing the life of faith. The objection "I do like to know that there is something going on" is, on this showing, at least partly met. Imperceptible to the senses is the prayer which we have been describing. The beauty of it is its secrecy; if there were standards by which it could be measured there would be no particular merit in its exercise. God's interests would be just as well served by a prayer of the senses. We know, however, that this is not the case. We know that God is better served by the act of contemplation than by the act of putting up a candle in His honour.

Both are prayer-acts, only one happens to be more pleasing to Him than the other. Of the two, moreover, it is the contemplative act that is the less pleasing to the person who prays.

"Ah *there* you are! You've missed the *whole* point. What you are thinking of is *contemplation*. That may be quite different; I wouldn't know. What *I* am thinking of are those periods of complete flatness which seem to come just when one would like to be able to pray properly — say after receiving Holy Communion — and which make one feel that the whole thing can't possibly be worth while or of the remotest interest to God. One is told to go on, of course, and one goes on. But nothing is going to persuade me that dryness, distraction, disinclination, temptation even, are what this spiritual prayer of yours has to show for itself. It's simply common sense to believe that putting up candles and singing hymns must be better than that." Pardon me, but even so....

INTERIOR PRAYER: ITS PROBLEM

NUMBERLESS PEOPLE GET in a generous routine of prayers each day; yet few practise real straightforward prayer. Numberless people go in for penances; few are downright mortified. Why is this? Are these people hypocrites, undertaking that sort of thing for the sake of vain glory? Surely not; for the most part they are in unquestioned good faith. Is it then that, consciously or unconsciously, they use their devotions as a substitute for recollection and their penances as a substitute for mortification? Certainly this would seem to be nearer the truth, but here again the element of good faith is not wanting in the substitutions. What happens in these cases is probably this: the prayer people are afraid to let go of their tried systems because they think they will be out of their depths and won't be sure any longer that they are doing anything at all in their prayer; the penance people are afraid that if they were to rely solely upon spiritual mortification there would be nothing to show for it. Thus in both cases what keeps them back from going on to what is better is really fear. The result is that they multiply their devotions and penitential practices in the hopes that they will never discover how unrecollected or how unmortified they are. The process is unconscious; it is the application, unsuspected, of the law of compensation. It would be difficult to point out their mistake to such souls, because if you were to tell them that what they are suffering from was a lack of generosity—which is what their fears amount to—they would bring forward their respective exercises and say "Surely there's no stinting here." That's the trouble. They won't recognise it, but it is a restricted service nevertheless.

Take the prayer people first. Like the disciples in the Gospel they labour the whole night through but take nothing: they will not launch out into the deep. They hug the shore. That safe familiar coastline, how compelling has been its attraction! "At least we can take soundings... and if the worst comes to the worst we can always get out and swim." The one thing that differentiates prayer, interior prayer, from any other exercise is that of course you *can't* take soundings. Nor will you trust to your swimming. The objections are perfectly valid—as objections, not as excuses. If you take a plumb-line to your prayer it either won't find, or if it does, will give you the wrong measurements. It is not that the waters are so deep, but that our apparatus is so inaccurate. The rules of navigation simply do not apply. Things like depths, speed of progress, currents, tides, visibility, storm and so on have a different meaning, are judged in new terms. Where there is relationship between two human beings there is common ground; exchange is effected by the use of symbols mutually understood. Where there is relationship between a human being on one side and God Almighty on the other, the intercourse is conducted on a completely different basis. I, the human member, can't help misunderstanding the terms, can't help forming wrong estimates of the exchange, can't help feeling out of my depth. Indeed I am out of my depth. I am in a different element altogether from what I have been used to, I am operating on another plane. So it's no good taking along my plumb-line, my X-ray, my stop-watch, my thermometer. I can't gauge the spiritual with the material. My feelings are the natural, my faith is the supernatural; feelings as an indication of success or failure are, in this matter of prayer, useless. To those souls, then, who like to feel the solid earth beneath their feet and who will not let go of vocal prayer or discursive meditation for the purer but less sensibly gratifying exercise to which God is possibly calling them, should be applied the words of the Gospel: "Why are you fearful, you of little faith?" Hand over the control to God; surrender yourselves; stop this business of forcing an emotion and leave yourselves free to accept whatever kind of prayer God sends you. Have no preconceived ideas as to how you ought to be praying. Content yourselves with trying to express, however inarticulately, your love of God. This love may be unfelt, this prayer may be unfelt; which is only what you would expect if the activity is to be one of faith. Faith in the last resort is the only answer, the only safeguard against miscalculation. Faith in prayer is not to be taken only as meaning confidence in obtaining results — this is the province of hope almost more than of faith — but as meaning also that trust which sets aside self and the evidence of the emotions.

With regard to the second group, the people who mistake penances for penance, there is a section coming later on in this book which attempts to deal with their problem. Enough to note here that the lines indicated above with reference to prayer are the lines to go upon in the matter of penance. Again faith. The mortification which goes on in the will, in other words, is of a far purer order than that which goes on in the senses. It doesn't show, and therefore is not as well liked. The penances of being surrendered to the will of God, of being accessible to the claims of man, of being serene under the fluctuating moods of self, are penances which have to be seen with the eye of faith if they are to be valued above the hair-shirt, the discipline, and the chain. If in our self-denial we are honestly looking for a self to deny — which not by any means everybody is prepared to do — we shall find far more of it inside, in the spirit, than outside, on the skin.

INTERIOR PRAYER: ITS CONDITION

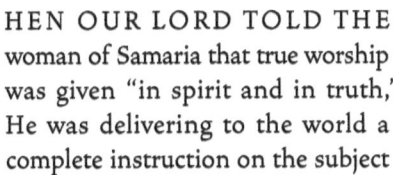HEN OUR LORD TOLD THE woman of Samaria that true worship was given "in spirit and in truth," He was delivering to the world a complete instruction on the subject of prayer. We have, in the foregoing snapshot articles on prayer, been dealing with that aspect of the love expression which is conducted in the spirit rather than in the senses; it is now the second requirement, worshipping in truth, that comes up for examination. That our prayers should be true is the condition without which they would not be prayers at all. Whether we pray with words, or mental pictures, or forced acts of the will, or aspirations of the heart, or with anything else whatever, the prayer is bound to collapse the moment we consciously strike a false note.

Whether in our dealings with God or with our friends it is never easy to be our true selves in every possible particular; certainly it must become less easy to be so if we use other people's words, ideas, and manners of expression. Granted that in any case we are liable to put on an act, isn't it nearer to the truth if we put on our own act rather than anyone else's? If we train ourselves to pray in our own way, using our own modes of communication, there is every likelihood that we shall not only come to a clearer understanding of God, but to a clearer understanding of our own selves; and that we shall cease accordingly from putting on acts.

If prayer is defined as the raising up of the mind and heart to God, it is of paramount importance that it should be *our* mind and *our* heart. It is difficult to see how those who rely solely upon prayers out of a book can avoid raising up other people's minds and hearts. Other people's minds and hearts are only of value to us when they exactly correspond to ours. If they do correspond, then by all means let them be raised. It is asking a lot, however, to believe that never are we out of tune with what we read, and that all our own private, intimate, peculiar, silly, fleeting sentiments can be aptly told in another's formula.

Whatever the medium it must be a familiar medium, even a flexible medium. Where the frame-work is awkward or rigid there will be gaps where the fit has not been exact, and it is into these spaces that distractions most easily find their way. The trouble is that we feel secure in the shelter of a frame, even if it is unyielding and belongs to someone else. We forget that because the relationship is one of the heart it must necessarily be peculiar, individual. In this life no prayer-form can be entirely comprehensive, but one that has been improvised to meet the needs of the moment is, however fumbling and incoherent when actually brought to bear, more appropriate to the soul concerned, more true, than anything bought in a shop. "Oh but I'm so inarticulate; if there's something there in print I seem to get confidence." Of course we are inarticulate when speaking the language of God — that is why He gives us the Psalms and other inspired prayers, so that we may make His language ours — but it is a delusion to imagine that being articulate or inarticulate matters either way. We shall not be held responsible for expressing ourselves badly, but only for not wanting to express ourselves at all. "Oh I want to express myself all right, but quite often there doesn't seem to be anything to express. And then if there's something there in print it seems a pity not to express that, even if it isn't absolutely what I happen to feel at the moment." If you have nothing to say, say so. God in any case has seen into your mind before you have, and if there is really nothing there for the time being He won't in the least resent your being honest about it. This is to be true, to be humble; it is what He wants. Certainly it would be a mistake under such circumstances to fall back upon a sentiment which looks the sort of thing one ought to feel, merely for the sake of finding something — incidentally something not quite true — to talk about. The object is not to keep up a constant flow. We are not asked to be raconteurs. One mouth, God has given us, to two ears. Yet the moment we start listening in our prayer for what God may have to say we begin to worry lest we should become illuminates, quietists, presumptionists and heaven knows what besides. The truth of it is that this waiting upon God in prayer, this prayer of simple regard which more often than not sees nothing but mist and blankness, both bores us and makes us uneasy. So we abandon it. We discard the fruits of prayer, and continue, with an industry not altogether free of self-esteem, to chew upon the pips. "At least you can get your tooth into a pip . . . pips can be chewed upon for ages." Quite so, but they are not very nourishing.

To conclude. Sincerity is one of the absolute essentials to prayer. Be true to the self which God has given you. Whatever your mood, your habit, your desire, *give Him that*. If you are drawn to ask for things, ask. Don't feel that the prayer of petition is a grasping sort of prayer, and that the only thing to do is to put up a prayer which looks very well on paper but which answers to nothing in your mind at the moment. Ask on, and give thanks to God for the grace to be praying about it. Whether He answers by giving or refusing what you want doesn't matter much: the main object has already taken place — He has got you into the frame of mind which sends you directly to Him about something which directly concerns you. This is the real achievement, this is you at your truest. This is praise of God as well as petition. It is taking Him at His word. Oscar Wilde once said that the great thing about prayer was that it should never be answered. "If it is," he explained, "it becomes a correspondence." Well, what if it does? The great thing about prayer is that it should be *made*. Even if afterwards it should become a correspondence and a not very selfless exercise, it at least has the merit of being genuine: it is genuinely ourselves. Correspondence with God? One might do worse.

INTERIOR PRAYER: ITS IDIOM

"ON YOUR SHOWING," IT might be objected by anyone who has followed this sequence of essays, "there is little or no need for vocal prayer. Even meditations seem to be ruled out. What about the Our Father, the Divine Office, the Mass? Would you do away with the considerations that accompany the rosary and the Stations? The drift of all this is tendentious, and savours faintly of something odd." If this objection is felt in so much as the slightest degree, there is only one remedy and that is to read the pages again. Nowhere has it been said that vocal prayer should be discarded or that meditation in some form or another need be eliminated. All that is claimed is that souls often debar themselves from a more profitable prayer by a very understandable but obstinate clinging to a form which, as regards the main business of their prayer, they have grown out of.* There is no state, however high, that can afford to say "No more vocal prayers for me," and considerations will always remain part of the general stock in trade. The difference as the soul mounts the way towards God is

---

* Far from growing out of the Divine Office, the soul, in proportion as it gets closer to God, grows into it.

merely that vocal prayers tend to become more mental, and meditations to become more simple. Neither is discarded or discouraged or despised; it is simply that the soul's main exercise is a more interior affair. There are times when this interior operation lets one down and one cannot do a thing. One tries but it is hopeless. This would be an occasion for falling back, for purposes of refuelling, to the more material assistances of vocal and discursive prayer. But even so, one should not do this too lightly; one should give the interior prayer a chance. A better approach would be to take hold of these material assistances and so to employ them as to make their expression more and more spiritual. Take the sentences of the Our Father and make of them the stuff of contemplation; take the mysteries of the rosary and speak through them, in one's own words or with no words at all, to God. The same may be said with regard to the Mass and the liturgy: follow it as you would follow the song of someone you love.

It would be the greatest of mistakes to imagine that the practice of interior prayer excluded the practice of any other. Prayer is not departmental. The element proper to prayer is the presence of God, and this is ministered to by every prayer activity whether exterior or interior. Interior prayer doesn't mean living inside oneself, shut in, *enfermé*. It means giving oneself to recollection, and this may involve the use of much vocal prayer, many considerations. As the recollection becomes purer and more habitual the mechanism becomes less complicated and cumbersome. The sweep is wider in extent and more penetrating in depth.

A glance at the conscience shows up as much material as previously a lengthy examination would have revealed, a resolve to love God more covers the ground which had hitherto to be furrowed by numberless resolutions, acts of faith and hope and charity come spontaneously from the heart and with little thought as to their verbal presentation. The spiritual life is no longer a business of careful wrapping up and unwrapping; it is the parcel and not the packing that is felt to be the main thing. The Divine Office and the Mass are given more value, not less. The psalms are prayed, not merely said. The Mass is lived, not merely heard. And of the Our Father it has been well pointed out* that it was not given to the disciples as a set formula to be learned off and recited but as a verbal illustration of the best way of praying. Not "This is your prayer; say it as well as you can" but "*Thus* shall you pray: Our Father..." When you pray, that is, treat your heavenly Father as a father... hallow His name... show Him that you want Him to rule... tell Him that you accept His will... ask Him for what you want, bread, grace, whatever it is... and so on. The way in which the disciples put their question to our Lord, the question which prompted the Our Father, shows that for all

---

* I forget by whom originally, Father Bede Jarrett certainly used the idea, but I think he said he had got it from someone else. Thus does a good thing go the rounds.

their ignorance of prayer they understood what we, for all our instruction, forget. They did not ask for a phrase or a series of phrases which would, if attentively repeated, get them what they wanted. They didn't ask for a model at all, they asked for a lesson. Not "Give us a prayer, Lord," but "Teach us, Lord, how to pray." And He did.

In the kingdom of prayer, then, there are many mansions. They vary in dignity. Not everyone is called to live in the most noble, but on the other hand not everyone who starts off in one of the more humble mansions is expected to go on living there for ever; he may be expected to make moves from time to time. The more spacious mansions are quite get-at-able and are crying out for occupants. The furniture from one mansion will not always suit another, but it need not be got rid of. Indeed *should* not be got rid of. The great thing to remember is that nothing must be clung to, whether furniture, mansion, or anything else. We go through life free with the freedom of the Father's house, which stands open-doored and inviting in the heart of the capital.

LOVE IN GENERAL

PRIEST SAID THIS TO ME the other day: "Love is the greatest menace to the state of grace that we have to deal with. It works exactly the same way in men as in women, in one country as in another, in one century as in another, in one class as in another. The thing is more trouble than it's worth. It's a racket." Priests who make statements of this sort, and who expect to be taken seriously, don't deserve to pronounce the vow of chastity.

Apart from the main error (which is that love's an infernal nuisance anyway) there is in the above pronouncement a number of minor misconceptions. These can be treated in a preliminary essay; the series which follows can be devoted to exploding the idea that love is more trouble than it is worth.

Love, like life itself, is largely what we bring to it. Bring God to love, and love is what it is meant to be; bring self, and love is dangerously near to lust. It is a confession of our own worthlessness to say that life or love is more trouble than it is worth. Life is a song only to those who are ready to sing; life is dreary only if we are dreary. Life mirrors our expression; it waits on us, not we on it. So with love. If we see love only as passion, it is because we are passionate; if we see it as part of God's poem to man, it is because we ourselves have fitted into its verses.

Bring God to love? But He is already there. God is love; human love is simply one side of it stretching out to the other. Human love is meant to tell us something of Divine love. This is primarily what it is for. To get the love of God right, we have only to learn the lesson from human love. The principle is the same. We don't have to juggle with terms and fool ourselves about motives; it's all there if we look. God's glory, to eyes which see straight, shines through human love as light through alabaster. Unfortunately our rebellious instinct has taught us to look for something else from human love, and everything in the world has conspired together to help our rebellious instinct in its search. The longing in human love can be cheapened, paraded, exploited and dragged into the limelight for all the wrong purposes until its original purpose has been lost sight of. The noble things of human love are made the subject of coarse jokes. Love's expressions are borrowed from their proper context and made to serve commercial ends: sex is found useful to trade with. Firms use sex to advertise their goods; they know the market value of excitement. There is a flame in human love, and the world knows that man is only waiting to play with the fire. The world goes out of its way to attract the souls of men and make them respond to each other's passion. While the heat of human love is remembered the purpose of human love is forgotten. So ready is man to yield to the wrong pressures of his nature that human love can fall short of being even human. Humanity was created good; love was created holy. Goodness and holiness are not afterthoughts.

To accept the world's view of humanity's purpose is not merely to miss the point intellectually; it is to sell the pass as regards the individual soul. In the same way to accept the world's view of love is not merely to waste, it is to debase. Sensation becomes the ruling factor. The world, with its press machine, can, whether to create the demand or to supply it, provide sensation by the yard. We exist on it. We can't work or talk or play unless we are stirred by it. In love we see it, and can see nothing else. We don't even look for anything else. "That's love," we say. It's nothing of the sort, it's an accompaniment to love. If love were that and that only, it could never be made to last. It could never take the weight of marriage. Sensation tires easily and has constantly to be fed. New satisfactions have to be found or all interest flags, and the love which was intended to be a lasting force for good becomes a jaded flabby sentiment incapable of rising to any heights beyond the selfishly romantic. Though the course of true love may seldom run smooth, it is not a series of leapfrog jumps from emotional crisis to emotional crisis. Man is inconstant enough apart from love, but if he gets his love wrong his inconstancy knows no bounds. It is his passion that leads him astray in his estimate of love, because it is his passion that burns itself out and leaves his love to cool. It is the man that is wrong, not the love. The love comes from God. God made human love right; man made it wrong. It was with Adam that love first went wrong. Then came Christ to take the wrong out of possibly wrongful things. Among these was love. That is why He gave marriage to man as a sacrament: He was taking the possible harm out of marriage. Man, alas, can put it back. By basing his love on passion, man can spoil God's plan for the second time. Man can reject the gift of marriage as a sacrament and accept it as something else; as something not wished for by God, but allowed. As something not merely weakening but destroying the purpose of marriage and love. Not merely weakening the bond between man's soul and God's, but spoiling it, breaking it to bits. Love is a coat without seam: you can't rend one part of it without rending the whole. If human love goes wrong, so also does love of God. Love, to get back to the assertion quoted at the beginning, may be a menace to the state of grace but it may also be the way into it. Love is not meant to be bracketed with mortal sin. Man has never quite recovered from the Fall and is still to be found stumbling. *But love is his success, not his failure.* If he comes to love with his eyes open he will see the inwardness of it. It won't be, for him, a racket.

"Love is the same in men and women, in this country as in that, in every period." Essentially it is the same because human nature is the same, but to say that the expression and nature of love run true to a universal form is wrong. A Latin loves differently from a Saxon for instance; the character of the thing, not merely the intensity of its expression, is different. The quality of a man's love is different, again, from a woman's. It isn't a question of degree but of kind. The man loves because he needs it, he has to be loved back. The woman because she rises to this need, because her nature responds. This is why men fall in love quite suddenly, before the woman has time to know whether she is responding or not. In the man it seems more grasping than in the woman, but it need not be so. For in the act of loving, man gives himself. The woman's part is essentially one of giving, but she too can grasp. Just as the man can be greedy for the woman's gift, so can she be greedy for his. But her part in love is to give back; his to give. Both generous but in different ways. If the races and the sexes give a different answer to the emotion of love, so also do the centuries. A generation such as the present, which has had its spiritual and moral values juggled with to such an extent that apart from the Christian code there are no sanctions left whatever, must inevitably love differently from the way in which men loved in the ages of the faith. It is not a question of mere fashion, but of faith. People who don't believe that there is anything in the sacrament of marriage cannot but love differently from those who do. The same applies to a generation. The powers of appreciation with regard to the whole problem of marriage and sex can so far decline that men of one generation may be "given up to a reprobate sense" such as men of another generation may not suffer from. The seed of love is there and is always the same, but it grows differently to the surface according to the ground it's in. The course of love is the course of life; the curve of each is the same. Our loves are measured by our lives. If we live for God we shall not love for self. Our love is largely what we bring to it.

MARRIED LOVE

"AREN'T YOU RATHER MIXING up sensation and sentiment?" it might be objected after reading the last section, "and whichever it is you mean, you won't find many marriages getting along without it." Sensation and sentiment are not the same thing but they lead to the same thing. Marriage is not expected to get along without sensation or sentiment; marriage is not meant to *rely* on them, that's all. They are the *etcetera* of love, not the reality.

Sensation and sentiment have the same origins and they can combine to produce the same result. Between them they can swamp the reason and stampede the will. Sentiment is a habit or a mood; sensation is a stimulus. "I was feeling sentimental, father, and then I got worked up. I don't know what it was . . . the music, the gins, the play we'd been to, the night . . . and it simply happened." This is the kind of thing the priest, sweating with misery, hears in the confessional. Sensation, then, is what works us up, and sentiment is what lets it. The two together canvas for the same votes in the general referendum, and if they get in they can dictate the wrong policy, define the wrong terms. They are hand in glove.

To say, however, that marriage should do without sensation or sentiment would be ridiculous. Human nature cannot manage without excitement of some sort. In marriage it must be the kind of excitement which can be controlled, which can be seen in proportion, which is not mistaken for the beginning and end of the whole business. In the same way sentiment, the romantic element as apart from the more immediately exciting, has also got to find its place in marriage. Marriage would be impossible without it. But again it must not be given the whole place. Nature craves for romance, and this is a perfectly healthy craving; but if it can enjoy nothing else, look forward to nothing else, talk about nothing else, read and think about nothing else, it is getting its emphasis wrong. Romance must serve love, not smother it. Romance (like its ugly sister, passion) has a way of cooling. But to deny romance to married life, to deny sentimentality even, is to ask for trouble. The very real need for something of this sort in the life of the human being is borne out by the way in which people flock to the cinema. Those whose lives are the most prosaic feel this particular urge the most. Their jobs and their homes are so dreary that they must find an outlet to sentiment somewhere, and the cinema provides it for the price of a seat. It is again the law of compensation. This, it should be added, must be understood as referring to ordinary harmless sloppy films about love and married life, and not to immoral ones which people go to for a different reason. The motives of the average cinema-goer are not easy to sift, but there is no reason to believe that they are not innocent enough. The harm done by films is accumulative rather than actual: it is the drift that is wrong. Nevertheless, the sentiment, however unhurtful, which is absorbed from the screen should be, ideally speaking, accounted for in other and less artificial ways. The nature of our lives ought to supply all the colour that we want; we should generate our own energy; we should be sufficiently creative to make romance out of reality, instead of having to rely for emotional release upon the borrowed experience of fiction. The home is the place where the married man or woman should be able to find expression, and if the family is so boring that it drives its members to the cinema it can only mean that the members aren't trying. I don't mean aren't trying to be romantic, but aren't trying to be members of the family. If they made it their purpose to build up that unit which we call the home they would discover all the romance and adventure and happiness that the world had to offer. They might not find much glamour. Life, again, is what we bring to it.

Sentiment, then, may be present in marriage — must be present in the initial stages or it would never get going at all — but it may not be allowed to take over the control. The balance must be maintained. Marriage is too big a thing to be stuck together by treacle.

If married love can be too cloying to last, it can also be too cold. Marriage is made for real people, not for lay figures, and to imagine that aloofness is the noblest expression of human love is a delusion. Inhumanity can never be the reflexion of what God has raised to the dignity of a human sacrament. To men and women with bodies has He given this sacrament. With bodies but with spirits first. Body wedded to body, but on condition that soul be wedded to soul. First, indeed, the union between soul and soul, then that of the flesh. Left in the body alone, marriage is an animal mating, beginning in an animal way and ending in an animal way. A thing that is finished with when the act has been performed and the desire has spent itself. Leave out the union of soul, and at best there is a business agreement or a scientific experiment, ceasing the moment the exchange has been effected or the biological effects achieved. The whole self must be wedded to the whole self. That is why there can be no divorce.

"You speak of union of soul," — this has been said to me by one about to marry — but the term is so vague. Two in one flesh I can understand; it is a fact that can be appreciated and experienced. But two in one spirit is outside ordinary perception; it is a too intangible idea. How do I know that I am so wedded in spirit to the one with whom I intend to spend my life that I may safely proceed to being wedded in fact?" The one is no less *fact* than the other; it is simply that the spiritual fact is less generally recognised than the other, and, by those who most need to benefit by its implications, less provided for. That two people should know a union of soul when they experience it should not be more extraordinary than that they should know that other union. The complete self-giving, sealed in the will . . . the surrender of heart, of independence, of separate wellbeing . . . mutual, permanent, unqualified. Is this so difficult to know? Cannot reason judge the signs? Cannot love provide the assurance? Or must man's inconstancy and ungenerosity prevent him from ever being certain.

On good intentions alone it would be hazardous to embark upon the state of matrimony. Many in the first gust of love are prepared to hand over everything with the completest confidence, and this is excellent as far as it goes, but they must know what they on their side are handing over, and what on the other side is being handed back. This sounds very calculating, but in actual fact it isn't: it is seeing how much you can give, not how little; how nearly you can rise to the height of the other's gift, not how much you can gain from it. There must, then, be this more-than-readiness to share what life promises with the chosen partner: there must be already a sharing, not yet of life but of common interest and ideal. Not identity of interest, but at least sympathy of interest. Not identity of ideal, but at least close similarity. Unless husband and wife hold certain mental qualities, tastes and ideas in common there is likely to be little to occupy them when the first thrill of their association has worn off. There must be more than each other and their affection to discuss; there must be more to do than sit about together. If this is true as regards subjects to talk about and ways of spending time, it is true as regards the more important issue, the question of holding the same principles. Since so much of their married life will depend upon making decisions and sticking to them, it is vital that husband and wife should be possessed of a twin conscience and as far as possible of a single purpose. How else can there be harmony when it comes to such things as forming a code of conduct in their marriage relations, agreeing upon how to bring up the children, allowing the place to be given to religion in their wedded life?

Two, then, in one flesh; two also in one spirit. The bond of self-giving sanctified by the sacrament. Generosity the beginning, the end, the condition. Sacrifice. Go to marriage for what you can get, and you are disillusioned; go for what you can give, and you find yourself immeasurably the richer for your gift. Go with your eyes open, looking for the beauty which is in marriage and prepared to pay the price. Looking for what love has yet to offer when the early blossom has blown away, and *still* prepared to pay the price. Costly must be love, else is it luxury. Hopeful, grateful, humble ... believing the best of love, not the worst ... as glad of its graces as of its pleasures ... ready always to acknowledge unworthiness in the face of a gift so excellent that none but God Himself could have devised its possibility.

MARRIED LIFE

ROM WHAT HAS BEEN SAID, then, God's purpose as regards marriage was not: "Here is an animal which is called man. His love life is largely animal. Since he can never be altogether tamed, I will give him a sacrament which will be able to save his soul, and which at the same time will give to his love the appearance of decency." No, God's plan was much more this: "Here is a reasonable creature with a lot of the animal in him. I will give man a sacrament which will appeal to the best instincts he's got, and which will, if he lets it, be an inspiration in his life and which will give him the opportunities of real holiness. If, however, his best instincts reject the offer, then his worst instincts will have it all their own way. *Then* the animal in him will be largely uppermost."

If there is similarity between the two statements, the similarity is purely superficial because they mean two quite different things. There is similarity between animal and human love, but they also are two quite different things: they have a different object. Let us make no mistake about this. Human actions may be the expression of human love, but this does not mean that they are animal in their nature. No action deliberately performed by rational beings is purely animal in origin. Human love can translate what is carnal to a noble level;

grace can elevate it higher still. Admittedly there is a perilous likeness between the animal and the human, and it is ever the business of the flesh to confuse the two. Either the flesh says "This is true love" when it isn't, or else "There's no such thing as true love" when there is. If it isn't exhibiting the best and pretending to be that, it is exposing the worst and saying that there's nothing else. The flesh on the subject of love is the last possible voice to listen to, but because it is so insistent it would be as well here to dispose of its claims.

That men and women mistake passing infatuation for the permanent reality is an only too common experience. Flirtations wear the make-up of love so as to appear as the real thing. Look closer and the essential quality is missing: there is no willingness to sacrifice, the attraction is not unselfish. The infatuated will give each other presents and will go out of their way to please each other. These are expressions, certainly, which may find some remote relation to the giving which is expressed in love; but if the gift is of kind only and not of self, if the gift is offered so as further to attract, if the gift is more of a bribe and reward than a symbol and manifestation, then, taken all in all, it can't be worth much. "Not the gift of the lover, but the love of the giver" is what matters. There may not be the least harm in a flirtation, and in any case people cannot help getting infatuated; all I am saying is that it is important to see where the attraction is coming from and what it is leading to.

Not perhaps so commonly but every bit as disastrously, the reverse is found to be the case, and what has been the authentic thing is judged, in the monotony of married life, to have been no more than a flirtation. "I thought we would go on being in love with each other... it seemed so clear then... but somehow it has all gone stale." The friend or the priest hears this sometimes within six months of the honeymoon. "So I suppose," concludes the disappointed soul, "we were never in love to begin with." No, don't suppose that. Don't say, either, that you are not in love with each other now. You probably are, but the love has gone deeper; and consequently there's less to show for it on the surface. Exactly the same thing happens in the business of loving God: there's no freshness, no fervour, no feeling. This is to be expected and made allowances for; it is no indication whatever that there has never been anything solid all along, or that, if there ever was, it has melted away. Where the day-to-day enters in, there is bound to be staleness sooner or later. Human nature, in the face of normality, drudgery, repetition, inevitably wearies. Being in love — by which I mean feeling in love as apart from simply loving — is largely fed by the element of discovery. Everything is new, everything a shock of surprise. That is the interest at first, that is the main attraction. Discovery and change: we thrive on them. Man sparkles where there is variety, but he is deadly dull in routine; and the sameness of married life underlines the poverty of his resources.

Yes, but what are people to do? If they may not part and if they cannot go back to where they started, the situation offers little consolation. Convinced that love has let them down, they think that the only thing to do is to maintain as little contact as possible and to keep up the fiction, even to each other as well as to the outer world, that all is more or less well. Before admitting that matters are as hopeless as this, the treatment applied in the spiritual order, which is parallel, should be seriously considered. Have you gone back on your original self-giving? Are you allowing into your life an affection, an activity, an absorption which you know to be upsetting the balance? Do you *want* to love? If the husband or wife, no less than the religious, can honestly say that in the will the original purpose has been stuck to, then there's no earthly reason to believe that love has petered out and that it will not reveal itself again in a somewhat different form. The point is that whether the love be human or divine, its terms assume a deeper meaning. Married people must learn that loving and being in love are not the same thing. And what is more they must not look down upon the one for not having the enthusiasm of the other. They will find that if they are faithful to the requirements of loving they will enjoy all the happiness, though again of a different order, which was ever experienced in those halcyon days of being in love. It is the qualification "of a different order" that chills them, that robs them of their hope. No need to. There are greater happinesses than, even, the surprise of falling in love. The content which comes from the knowledge that one's love is returned, and has been returned over a period of many years, must outweigh for sheer gratification absolutely anything. Add to this not only the certainty (which in spite of everything comes eventually) that this mutual exchange of all that matters most will continue until one or other die, but also that the love is being reduplicated in others, in the family. Falling in love holds only the promise; loving enjoys the reality. So also in the spiritual life: serenity more than makes up for the lack of sensible devotion. One's love of God is there, fixed in the will, and God is returning it. If the manner of the exchange is not what we thought in the beginning that it would be, this is not because the exchange is going wrong but because we thought wrong in the beginning. Add to this happiness the knowledge that other souls are learning from us what we have learned, that but for this union between my soul and God's there might never have been new members to His spiritual family, and the joys of married life are heard to echo in the heart of the religious.

The married man can, heaven knows, be excused for mistaking the promise which his earlier experience held out. Everything that he has heard and read of love since he was a boy has had to do with falling into, not keeping up with, love. The reason he has heard little of love as a life is because this aspect of it has hardly any dramatic or literary interest. The story, from the publisher's point of view, is over. The "human" page is turned, and nobody bothers about the rest. It becomes middle-age at once. The result of hearing so much about how it begins and so little about how it goes on is that not only is the wrong interpretation assumed but the wrong remedy applied. (I don't mean separation, because this is no remedy at all.) Instead of finding the solution in each other's happiness, they look for it in trying to recapture the atmosphere of their engagement. Parties and presents and meeting people all day long had been so amusing then, why not try them again now? A husband will conscientiously plan numberless ways of drawing back love to his own and his wife's heart, but he will completely miss the right way. She in her turn will spend endless trouble in making herself look beautiful for her husband's sake, not realising that by now he loves her for much more than for her appearance. These cross purposes in a marriage are a tragedy. Artificial compensations never work. It is the same as regards the treatment of the children; parents will arrange expensive ways of amusing their family, when what the family really needs is to amuse itself in its own way—as a family. If husband and wife will only believe that the solution has got to come from inside and not from outside, there would not be so many mistakes. The man thinks that running the house is turning his wife into a bore so he pays someone else to do it. The woman thinks that it's dull for her husband to have nobody but herself and the children to entertain him, so she fills the house with people and packs off the children to the nursery. He and she are both at their worst in the mornings, so let them not have breakfast together. One or other hates the country, so what is the point of their going for a holiday together? "The theatre bores me . . . but of course you go." "They've asked us both, but you loathe them so I'll go." "The children want a picnic, but there's no reason why we should go." Gradually the whole thing drifts. It's bound to — if members of what is meant to be a single unit insist on living their own lives. In marriage more than in anything else giving is the unifying force, and there is no giving if there is no sharing. Sharing doesn't only mean taking your slice of the cake. The Christian ideal is practicable only on Christian terms. The flame of love will die down and finally flicker out if it is not coaxed and blown upon from every angle. Neglect it and out it goes. Smother it and it doesn't stand a chance. The wonder is not that so many marriages come to grief, but that so many, seeing what mistaken notions people have about it, don't. Very few would come to grief at all if husband and wife understood at the outset that marriage was going to mean doing a lot of dull things and doing them together . . . and that *in* doing them they would find their common happiness. Not separate happinesses, but common happiness. But people can't be persuaded to look upon happiness as a by-product, as an overflow.

We have seen then how easy it is for an attachment of the moment to masquerade as the affair of a lifetime, and also how easy it is for the affair of a lifetime to assume, when seen retrospectively, the colours of an infatuation. From the second of these errors it is logically only a step to go one further and accept the suggestion that there is no upright love anywhere and that the whole business is straightforward earthy passion.

As put to us the idea is not so cynical as here stated. It even wears the disguise of humility and sincerity. "I see how low my nature is, and I frankly admit it. This cant about spiritualising love only makes people into hypocrites. A man should face facts, and go about his married life in a strictly realist way." This is not humility, it is a betrayal. It is not realist, it is just simply wrong.

If it were true that expressions of love had no source save in the animal, then it would be equally true to say that other expressions of other human instincts owed their origin to the brute. Beastly we may be, but we are not as beastly as that. Why take nature at its lowest instead of at its highest? We belong to that order of created nature which can subdue the species which comes below us on the list. Subdue it and benefit by its service. Why, under pretence of humility and forthrightness, debase ourselves so low that brute creation masters us? In the matter of love, we are either lords or slaves. "Not at all," says your gross materialist, "we go about, passion and I, hand in hand." There is no conflict here because there is no ideal. The human, the spiritual, the divine, is present and waiting, but the animal has gained the day.

If love be thought of in terms only of the flesh, what a travesty must be the mood in which love's crowning expression is performed. That act which God intended as a sacred seal upon a union He has blessed, that pledge of mutual dedication to be approached with reverence and awe, that fulfilment of a promise divinely ordained . . . how does man acquit himself of this? The mind sickens at the thought of what the dispositions of one who holds unChristian views may sometimes be. And even pagan-tainted Christians, how do they approach? Contemptuously? Coarsely? Even drunkenly? Men and women have before now taken too much to drink on the night of their marriage for perhaps no other reason than that they should not show self-consciousness in the performance of so intimate an act. With others — and these the more guilty — the act has arisen out of drunkenness. What would even the most indifferent Catholic think of the man who came on drunken and uncertain feet to receive the Holy Eucharist? The Blessed Sacrament is not the only Sacrament which is blessed. Holy Communion is not the only union which is holy. Apart from the desecration, apart also from the effect upon the souls of those who so embark upon their union, what of the fruits of such a marriage? What of the child? Parents are sometimes puzzled by the evil which they see in a growing boy or girl. Where does it come from? "I wasn't like that," they say, "when I was that age." Perhaps not, but were you like that when the child was begotten and conceived? That was the moment when the relationship between the two of you began. What you were at the age which the child is now has no bearing. The very word "conceived" is a reminder of the part the parents play: a new character is conceived, designed, fore-moulded almost, by what has gone before the birth. Terrible, but wretchedly understandable, is the sullen resentment of Housman's lines:

> *The day my father gat me,*
> *His thoughts were not on me.*

Were they not? They should have been. You mustn't be too hard on him: the thought of responsibility has its work cut out to compete with the thought of pleasure. But what is the result? Lonely and self-excusing is the reproach of the next generation. And man is fool enough to ask "Where does this evil come from?"

Love may indeed be weighted by the flesh, but God has so appointed that the pressure may be countered by the spirit. Love can rise. Love can take the flesh with it in its ascent. Love — the whole of love and so the human love as well — must find its proper home in God.

"Let those who exercise their privilege, Lord God, treat it for what it is: a trust from Thee. Not as earth-bound but heavenly... so let them render thanks when it is done." Were we to pray no other prayer but only this for the welfare of mankind, we would be doing no mean service to the age in which we live.

MAINLY FOR SCHOOLMASTERS

IF THERE IS ONE MAN MORE than another who is liable to mistake the means for the end it is the schoolmaster. He is inclined to get his directions just sufficiently wrong to make the whole difference. He mistakes instruction for education, legislation for authority, knowledge for wisdom, tyranny for control, and a whole host besides—not to mention those more personal judgments which mistake toughness for courage, subservience for obedience, affection for sentimentality, high spirit for ostentation, shyness for complacency, and generosity for extravagance. The list can be extended indefinitely. In fact wherever you come across innumerable carts drawn up before a horse you will know that in all probability a schoolmaster has put them there. And the chances are it will be the wrong horse. Why is this? Is it because so much of the schoolmaster's concern is to do with the keeping of rules and the passing of exams that he forgets what purpose it is that rules and exams are meant to serve? Is it that in dealing with a generation not his own he is more conscious than he need be of the mental substitutions that are required? Is it that on account of the numbers who pass through his hands he is inclined to generalise, and get his generalisations wrong? This last is the most probable explanation, but even so *why should he* get his generalisations wrong? Ah, surely the answer to this one lies in the fact that from the moment the man sets foot on the quicksand territory of the school it is dinned into him that above all he must not allow himself to be put upon. "The little beasts will swing it," he is warned. Look at him as he wipes his spectacles outside the classroom door. Watch him grasp those books with hands of steel. Hear him kick his chair as he mounts the dais. We know that however self-confident he is, whether in appearance or in reality, that man is suspicious, on the defence, ready to pounce. Of course he is, he has to be. No blame to him. But what it means is that any generalisations which in later years he allows himself to make—and schoolmasters allow themselves this luxury more than most—will be coloured by that early and slightly untrue attitude of mind. Unless a man is of highly independent spirit, unless he is a man of vision, unless he believes in human nature to a degree of almost extravagant idealism, he will be prone, as he stands back and views the filing hundreds who have come under him, to consider the less significant, the less essential. Between them the factors of time and quantity can have a hardening effect upon the soul. Inelastic we mostly are by nature, and still more inelastic we tend to become with years. We have seen so much; every sort of experience has been ours; within our particular field there is nothing we don't know. "Boys? Boys? I've dealt with 'em all my life." Association with the characters of others, even if they be fine characters, is not enough of itself to turn us into idealists. Unless we are careful, it sometimes turns us into disillusionists. It's the force of numbers and the repetition in time: we feel that there's nothing new enough to be lovely; we are no longer capable of being surprised—even by the beautiful. If belief in humanity is the first condition of dealing with the young, then this is precisely where the test comes in. First of all, have we boundless confidence in human nature as a whole? Secondly, in the inherent goodness of every member of it? The good may be delayed, obscured, misdirected, undervalued, and in a hundred ways rendered inoperative, but the point is that it's *there*. All it wants is the grace of God and a flick along the right lines, and it will answer to its name. God can be responsible for the grace, it is for those who are engaged in education both to provide the right lines and to propel their young people along them. Perhaps not propel so much as invite.

In an age when parents are more than ever ready to hand over to others the responsibility of bringing up their children it is vital that those in whose favour the power is abdicated should know their job. Should know it, moreover, as a vocation rather than as a career, putting the emphasis on the inward rather than on the outward. On the supernatural more than upon the natural. Even *naturally* speaking it is obvious that the closed mind, the hardboiled attitude such as we have described which card-indexes the lowest instead of the highest, the superficial instead of the real, the quality that imposes itself instead of the one that has to be looked for, misses the most worthwhile in youth, but what does it not miss *supernaturally*? A man may not be so much to blame for making mistakes which are due to common prejudices and common acceptations, but he is very much to blame indeed for not giving what is his supernaturally to give. This is the kind of mistake he may not make. If he withholds the fruits of his training, of his experience, of human intuition and sympathy, he is behaving badly enough; but if he fails to communicate the fruits of his faith he is frustrating the purpose of his vocation. The Christian who has the care of the young stands at a crossroads, and is in a position to point pretty much in any direction he chooses. It is a frightening responsibility. Does he point towards Christ, or towards Christian culture, or towards culture without Christ, or towards himself? Almost anywhere on the journey he can take out the map and focus the attention of his followers upon the non-important or the relatively non-important. For one who wins the affection of many — or for the matter of that even of one — there is always the danger that he will keep the loyalty for himself and not refer it further. The greater betrayal is this if it is in virtue of his state as a priest or religious that the allegiance was initiated: he is exploiting his office for selfish ends.

A spiritual man may give himself with all his heart to souls, but if the response which this gift evokes is no more than a personal one returned to *him*, and if he allows it to remain so, he is reaping in terms of self only: his work is not God's.

Young people are not shepherded by Providence into our sphere of influence to be taught out of a book or to be won to the admiration of our personalities. Both these elements may come in, must come in, but they are not primarily what education is for. Through our books and through ourselves we impress upon the minds of others what we believe it to be best for them to know. Just as the books must have something positive to contribute, so must we. What is our stock in trade? No one can give more than he has got, and if one in authority is spiritually impoverished, the work which he does for souls will be impoverished accordingly. We can't awake enthusiasm by pretending to be enthusiastic, we can't point to a beauty which we don't see. Only if Christ is a reality to us can we preach Christ, only in the measure that we live the Christ-life can we effectively teach it to others. "Preach Christ? Teach Christ? But that isn't in the terms of the agreement." No, but it is in the terms of the vocation . . . and you don't have to do it from the pulpit or by commenting on the Gospel text. What is remembered by those who come under you is *you*, and if you are, like St. Paul, an *alter Christus*, you are training minds as they are meant to be trained. They will remember Christ. They will remember you too, but that does not matter. Even the fact that they will remember you for the best you had to give them instead of for the worst, must not, for you, be allowed to matter. The only thing that weighs with you is the memory which you give to them of Christ.

MORE ABOUT EDUCATION

IN THE FOREGOING SECTION it was argued that youth carries with it into the world what we, the elders, put of ourselves into the work of its upbringing. As in art so in education: the things which stick in people's minds after reading a book or seeing a play are those things into which the author has put most of himself. It may be the plot, or the ideas, or the characters, or certain of its lines. "Out of ourselves we can never pass," says Oscar Wilde; "nor can there be in creation what in the creator was not." The work of education is as near to that of creation as anything can be. It may not be the making of something out of nothing, but it is often the making of something out of material which, on the superficial view, doesn't amount to much. The test of education is what it can make of precisely this material—rather than what it can make of what is promising anyway. Given the right soil any fool can grow a mushroom; given a glass bowl any fool can stock it with goldfish: it requires the gardener to produce mushrooms from peat blocks, the conjurer to produce goldfish from a bowl which is empty. The readiness with which apparently poor material can respond is sometimes frightening, and the responsibility upon those who are in a position to give it something to respond to is all the greater.

This responsibility is evaded in one of two ways. Either the schoolmaster fails to produce in *himself* the positive thing which he should be giving out to others, or he is afraid to ask of others what he knows to be worth asking for. In either case both his instinct and his memory of how he himself used to feel about these things as a boy tell him that so far as co-operation goes the deficiency is not on the side of youth. The barriers which mostly divide us from others are not those which we have learned in childhood to put up; far more often they are the defences of middle age. Where the young are sometimes handicapped by shyness (which need not always be a bad thing), their seniors are at a greater disadvantage: for them the obstacles are laziness, fear, selfishness and suspicion — which *are* bad things. "Give 'em common sense," says the pedagogue of thirty years' experience; "teach 'em the set subjects and the moral law; let 'em get on with those, and don't let's have all these circus tricks about higher spirituality for the young. These creatures are the wrong age for subtleties. Won't understand a word. In one ear, out the other." Such an approach is bluff, sensible, possibly well-meaning, and entirely wrong. The conclusion to be drawn from such an attitude cannot but be stultifying. What can youth learn from a doctrine which does not invite to a level higher than that on which it already stands? Must we always understand a subject before we are given the chance of benefiting by it? "Take care," says the other pedagogue to his colleague in the commonroom; "don't let yourself be got at; those young devils are just trying us out. Relax for half a minute, and they've got you." Thus from the first day in the classroom (when he mistakes curiosity for guile and simplicity for secrecy), the unfortunate young master goes barking up the wrong tree for the whole of his teaching career.

Few things paralyse effort so completely as caution, and where there is failure in education it is nearly always due to the over-exercise of human prudence. It is in the nature of man to be afraid of giving everything either to God or to God's creatures. For the perfection of education there has to be this giving to both God and man. A man who has the care of youth should have the courage to "give himself away" — which supposes that he has something to give. More than anything else it is fear which keeps schoolmasters from either attaining to or assisting the sanctity which their profession is perfectly designed to promote. Fear is one of the least recognised forms of selfishness, and though a man may be unsparing of himself in the work which he gives to education he may yet at the same time, through a selfish dread of committing himself, be missing in one of the first essentials of his service.

The small-minded man is so dominated by the established order of education that he will not risk disturbing its surface even for the sake of the souls which education is meant to serve. He becomes wedded to the secondary consideration. He sees the wood so clearly that in case he should lose sight of it for a moment he dare not look at the trees. The result is that all along he has to sacrifice personality to system — his own personality being the first to suffer. He dare not cut the cloth to any but the official pattern of coat, he dare not temper the wind to the shorn lamb, he dare not break the traditional mould. The coat won't fit? Then the boy must be altered to suit it. The shorn lamb is shivering? Then the sooner it grows some more fleece the better. The mould is ruining what it has been given to mould? Then the material must be hopeless. "Let him go on with his education at home (or abroad, or not at all), but he's no use to us." *Use* to us! Is this what people go to school for — to be of use to the system? If ever there was a cart before a horse it is here.

But good education is not merely the avoidance of bad mistakes. Good education finds a void and fills it, finds something warped and straightens it. The formation of character is not so much a matter of commanding and punishing; it is more a matter of providing for what is needed and substituting for what isn't. There is little to be gained from telling boys not to do this or that, not to read this or that, unless you supply them with something better to do and read. There are those who are perfectly satisfied to have created a vacuum. These will never lead or inspire;

at best they will only restrain. As the boy's intellect has to be fed with knowledge, so his character has to be given something to bite on — principles, positive remedies, an active lead. I have seen a man who had a genius for youth so work for the success of a boy whom everyone else had written off as a bad character that the finished product was not merely a brand rescued from the burning but a powerful influence for good. The common judgment had been true but only half true; what the discerning mind had seen was that the whole truth might emerge in the end. The youth's affections were seen to be all wrong; but where another would have said "Stifle your emotions: they are rancid and rotten," this man said "Train your emotions: they are capable of working right." He showed that where love has been responsible for breaking up a life, love must be made to mend it again. People need to be given something to do with their love which is good instead of bad. But it needs courage to educate in this way; it needs also perseverance and boundless belief in youth. There must be a vision and purpose which is ready to transcend the ordinary measurements of convention and custom and common sense. The schoolmaster must rise above the schoolmaster mentality. His action must not be determined by "What would my colleagues say? What would the governing body say? What would the rest of the school say?" None of this is at all to the point. The only question which he need bother about is, "What is *here and now* the best for this particular soul?" The problem concerns someone who is made in the image and likeness of God. If this is so, the only question worth asking is, "What would *God* say?"

Wide-eyed, then, and prepared to regard each new problem as a new problem: such is the attitude of the Christian educationist. Nothing doctrinaire, nothing borrowed, nothing set. Once we see people as problems which we have come across before, we stiffen. Education is something more than the effect of a theory upon a boy or girl. It is even something more than the fruit of past experiences which bear some relation to this particular boy or girl. It is, in the last analysis, the effect of one individual character upon another individual character. Character is not conveyed by quoting precedent or reading out of a book. The only effective medium, the truly conducting quality, is character. For this there must be sympathy, understanding, confidence. Prejudice cuts at the roots of the whole thing; preconception forces into a readymade channel. Education has to be personal or it is nothing. Relationship, or it is nothing. How else can there be communication? All work for others must rest upon the impact of individuality upon individuality. How shall they learn who hear only words? How, even, shall they *listen*? It will mean nothing to them. (You are right, sir, and thank you for the phrase . . . in one ear and out the other.)

FATHER BEDE JARRETT

THE REASON FOR INTRODUCing biography into a book of essays is because in this instance the subject of the biography bears out the general idea of this book. If any man's attitude towards life was open-eyed, it was Father Bede Jarrett's. Another reason lies in the fact that had there been no Father Bede there would certainly have been no book. By his life—by his work as well, but more especially by his life—he taught me what I have tried to put into these pages. He opened windows. This was the important thing. All I have had to do since is to try and describe the view.

When a man sees life and loves it, his first instinct (perhaps even before wanting to give thanks for it) is to wonder how he can share his vision and experience with other people. This was the whole of Father Bede's problem, a problem which he went on progressively solving till the moment of his death.

To say that someone loves life is often to say that he loves the good things of life: that he sees pleasure everywhere, and picks it up with both hands. Father Bede's love of life extended far beyond the idea of pleasure. In loving life, he loved it as a unity: pains and pleasures taken equally in the gift. Wide-eyed though he was in looking at happiness, he was by no means blind to life's misery. He knew all about that. This is surely one reason why his idealism was so true: it had to be built up, brick by brick. About his view of life there was no evasion or self-deception or unreality. He loved living, particularly living for other people, and he knew that there could be no full living without the Cross. He loved people to be alive, he loved to be alive himself, and his first demand of literature and art and education and work and conversation and the religious life was that these things should be alive. His own vitality inspired and demanded vitality. I remember telling him when I was in a black mood that there was nothing I wanted so much as to die, and he simply could not believe that such a thing was possible. "This isn't you," he told me, "you can't be serious." That anyone should want to surrender his hold on life, unless from the motive of sacrifice, was to him inexplicable. It could not be a true feeling: it could not conform with what was in the mind. In the mind there could be no love of death, and the feelings must be made to follow suit. To him life was worth while all the time; worth while also were enterprise, effort, nature, study, games, and above everything people — all people irrespective of their abilities, beliefs or class. Whatever came his way was such a positive reality to him that any sort of negation was more than a mere waste; it was almost a rebellion, an evil. One felt that to undervalue a good thing in his presence was to give him pain; one felt that misappreciation was gross ingratitude. Though he understood every other temptation known to man and sympathised with it, I very much doubt if he could ever have understood the temptation to suicide. He would have forgiven it and made excuses for it, but not seen the point of it.

Strong personalities affect us in two different ways. First there is the great man whom we feel we want to accompany through life even if it means being dragged along at his chariot wheels. We give to his powers of will and judgment our unqualified admiration and allegiance; we recognise in him a force which amounts almost to an additional sense and which may not be resisted; we are awed, rather than drawn, into making a return. Then there is the other kind of great man whose greatness is nothing like as impressive at first sight, and whose influence pervades rather than imposes. To him we feel bound rather by the harmony which is found to exist between the two natures, ours and his, than by any sort of necessity. By kinship rather than by absorption. This second greatness is more stimulating than the other because it elicits energy from the individual instead of merely pumping it in from outside. It is less spectacular but of a higher order. Not so arresting but more productive. Father Bede's greatness was of this second kind. He never dominated one; one was never exhausted by him. I have said above that he demanded vitality: he did, but not in the sense of exacting it. He never exacted anything from his friends or from life. His nature was such that it invited a generous response, which it almost invariably got. He raised people from their level to his. There was accordingly nothing oppressive about this, nor did one feel that one had to be constantly on tiptoe to reach the standard he required of one; the fledgling had to make none of those frantic efforts at flight. The unselfconscious and perfectly natural response which people made to his lead was perhaps the greatest proof of his genius.

In writing of a man with marked individuality, and of one moreover whose contact with his world was intensely personal, the biographer has to write about Father Bede as he sees him. Not necessarily, that is, as others see him. I say this because in the many presentations which (I hope) are being handed down, mine may quite well be different from anyone else's. If so, it is not because Father Bede played different parts before different people, or that he played a special part before me, but because the very different people who have so far recorded their appreciations of him have variously, in the light of their own personalities, interpreted the same part. To quote an axiom which Father Bede was himself fond of quoting: "Everything we know comes to us according to the dispositions of our receiving mind." Which is precisely why he saw so much beauty in life: the setting was already there, in his own mind. Life, to repeat again and again, is what we bring to it.

It is not mere fancy to think of Father Bede's many friends returning to the memory of the man whom they knew, each with his own picture, each with a different impression of him. I once showed a photograph of Father Bede to a friend of his. It was after his death, and the friend said: "But I don't remember him like this. Here he is smiling. To me he was much more the cool, controlled, poised man of vision: the ideal religious superior." I, on the other hand, remember him as smiling. Again, when there was a question of introducing his Cause in Rome, another friend of his (perhaps "admirer" is a better word than "friend" in these connexions) told me that the sanctity side of Father Bede's character had never really struck him. "Come to think of it, he *was* holy... only I suppose he kept it dark." To me, on the other hand, his holiness was — though he certainly did his best to keep it dark — so incandescently obvious that if one wasn't talking about it the whole time it was simply because one was taking it for granted.

Perhaps it is in the nature of the kind of greatness which elicits from within rather than impresses from without that it is variously interpreted by those who come across it. Different people see their hero in terms of their own appreciation. Not in terms of their own *experience* — because their failure is more revealing to them than their achievement — but in terms of what they are looking for. When you see a man putting those things first which you yourself want to see put first, there is at once a link. Whether or not you are an exponent, or even a representative, of what you rate as being of first importance, you know the quality when you see it. To any religious the sanctity of Father Bede must have stuck out a mile.

Admiration of others, whether it takes the form of hero-worship or love, comes about in one of two ways. Either you find vested in an individual the qualities which you most admire, or you come across an individual who reveals to you qualities which you now find to be admirable. It is a matter of which comes first in the order of time: your assessment of values, or the person who teaches you how to assess your values for you. The second of these is probably the more common experience. Certainly in my own case I found the man first and the qualities afterwards. Boys take character very much for granted, and until Father Bede came on to my horizon I don't suppose I had considered what were the qualities in particular to be admired in a man. Yielding to an influence involves discoveries of every sort: one discovers a range of possibilities not only in the other person but in oneself. It is as if vibrations were set ringing in the soul. One feels the same answering chord which one experiences, though in a lesser degree, when coming across true poetry. In the presence of first-class poetry one grasps the other's emotion and finds that in fact it has been one's own all along, never expressed up till now; one had never realised its possession. It is much the same in this kind of friendship, where you have ignorance and devotion on the one side and infinite understanding on the other. With the coming of Father Bede, vista after vista opened out, and one found, as in Chesterton's *Coloured Lands*, that they were views of one's own back garden.

At the age of fifteen, mine was one of those middling minds which are intelligent enough to see the flaws in most things and not intelligent enough to see the perfections in any of them: it saw objections everywhere and solutions nowhere. I was not so much the grumbler, however, as that flashy kind of cynic who is common enough in the fifth forms of every generation. My one idea was to spread devastation with the blistering quality of my wit. This ambition was doomed to disappointment because I had no conversation and could not remember epigrams; nevertheless by dint of industry I was getting better at it when Father Bede came my way and changed the direction for me. In his philosophy there was no room for cynicism, however amateur, so this particular pose had to be dropped. It was not consciously driven out, it was simply replaced by what was found to be more absorbing. Then followed the opposite extreme: a period when, having learned that life was an adventure, the boisterous exhibitionist took the cynic's place. Zest was the note now struck, but it was an artificial note. If the critic had left his place in the stalls it was only to appear on the stage before the footlights. This was a bad patch, but here again the general ethos of the Father Bede influence came to the rescue, hinting at the vulgarity of attracting attention to a self that could not hold the attention once it had attracted it, hinting at the vulgarity of attracting attention *at all*. Here was a man at one's elbow who had a great deal that the world might look at with profit, and to whom at the same time display was abhorrent. Exhibitionism in the face of this humility became impossible; it was no longer any fun to show off; the phase petered out. It would be too long and too boring to recount the series of blunder-zones from which, without fully realising what was going on at the time, Father Bede led me. There was the scruple period, the isolationist period, the misunderstood period, the sentimental period, and the rough stuff period. This covered a considerable portion of my life, as well as taking up a considerable time in his.

It is difficult, in accounting for the occasions when a man has steered a follower away from danger, to avoid the idea of censoriousness. It was not that Father Bede showed active disapproval, and certainly he was never even remotely discouraging, it was simply that his whole bearing both towards life in general, and towards that aspect of it which one happened to be exploiting at the moment, was such that fallacies came to be exposed and new ideas introduced. The thing began to look childish or pointless or sordid, and one wanted to do something else which was better: something probably which he was doing supremely well. This must surely have been the experience of many. We never felt that contact with him was flattening, was preventing us from having an amusing time; we felt that the more we saw the overall picture from his point of view, the less flat and the more amusing time we would have. His own radiating gaiety ensured us this.

The joy both of achievement and of sheer good spirits was abundantly evident in Father Bede. He delighted in doing things and getting others to do them. The talent-sense which certainly he himself possessed he would go to endless trouble to awaken in us, showing by his own pleasure that satisfaction must inevitably follow the right use of a gift; follow even the unskilled use. He would encourage me to go on writing verse although the stuff I showed him was, I can see now, drivel. It was the same with my drawing, with my proposed speeches, my plays, and later on my sermons. They were all awful, and I have no doubt that other people's were too, but he made us go on, giving us suggestions and often doing the hack work himself. He was creative, and wanted others to know the joy of creative work; but besides the joy of it he knew the strain of it, and about this he taught us as well. "Whatever it costs you, *do it*." What perhaps he didn't realise — and if he did, I doubt if he let himself enjoy the idea — was that his greatest, and most costly, creative work lay in his dealings with us, his disciples. He was making real people out of dummies. Whether he dwelt on this in his mind or not, the very use of his talent in this direction cannot but have given him joy. His legacy was not so much his books or his buildings but his friends. Whether among his own subjects, the members of his order, or among outsiders like myself, the greatest work he did was in the way of individual formation; and the gratification which comes of signing your name in people, even though those people will die and your name will be forgotten, is greater than that of leaving your signature on anything else.

Of that other joy, the gladness of the moment, there would be less reason to speak were it not for the fact that spontaneous gaiety was so much part of his composition that any account of him which left it out would be lamentably incomplete. If there is one memory which his friends will carry with them it is that expression of his which used to light up his whole face quite suddenly, as if a switch had been turned on. Looking back there seems to me nothing more characteristic than this lightning alteration which took place when either something funny struck him or he wanted someone else to enjoy what he was enjoying. The quick laugh which was almost a yelp, the sudden raising of the eyebrows and flash of teeth, the momentary jerk of shoulders: this combination must have shaken many of us out of our pomposities and depressions. Those who didn't know him well might have mistaken his lightheartedness for frivolity, and people have been heard to wonder whether there was any of the asceticism such as we associate with really holy souls under all that obvious merriment. The reason why Father Bede's asceticism was compatible with his joy is because it was itself joyous. He laughed at the cold (from which he suffered more than most men); he laughed at the lack of sleep (which for years it was his lot to put up with). He never spoke about his health or his nerves, though one knew long before his death that both were being taxed far beyond ordinary endurance. His rule of poverty was "to give up everything you can do without," and this he interpreted strictly, denying himself books (which he took out from the library when he wanted them, instead of keeping a collection of his own), extra clothes, newspapers, comfortable chairs, good luggage, photographs and so on. The only time I ever saw him drink anything stronger than coffee was when both of us, extremely hot and thirsty, drank champagne. There was, incredibly enough, nothing else. If austerity is looked for in the life of Father Bede there is plenty to be found in the amount of work he managed to get through, in the number of hideously unpleasant journeys he had to make, in the vast quantity of people he had to see. He admitted that he hated travelling, but he used it as he used everything else as a heaven-sent opportunity: on his journeys he prayed and worked and read. In his refusal to waste time Father Bede's mortification must have reached a very high degree indeed. His was a nature that tended naturally to the greatest legitimate liberty, and yet he tied himself down to what was as rigid a discipline as the circumstances of his life would allow. Father Bernard Delany tells how, when away on his preaching tours, Father Bede would follow wherever possible the regular time-table of his community at home. I myself remember coming upon him in a station waiting-room where we had arranged to meet on an occasion when our journeys crossed, and finding him with pencil and paper. "Letters?" I asked. "No," he replied, "the history of Europe." In Basingstoke station.

More significant even than the prodigious output of writing there is the irrefutable testimony, if proof of a man's mortified spirit is required, of his unfailing accessibility. Never dismissive, never appearing in the least bored or tired or strained, never flustered or jumpy or preoccupied, he seemed to give the impression of having nothing else to do but see to your particular problem. You felt, quite wrongly, that time didn't matter to him. You felt — he made you feel — that you were the one person he had been wanting to see. This was not just the case with regard to his friends; everyone felt it. All felt that here was a person who actually wanted one . . . who apparently liked listening . . . who would sympathise and laugh and give advice and ask one to come again . . . the chance was not to be missed. No wonder he was imposed upon, weighed down, sucked dry, sent for at impossible hours and from all over the country. There he would be, fresh, unhurried, perfectly mannered, gay. Then, the moment he was free again, he would be back to his books and his correspondence. To some the habit of answering letters by return of post is no hardship; to Father Bede it was. It must have meant that for days on end he had absolutely no leisure at all: he could never really relax. This was what killed him. Outwardly so serene and smooth, he was mentally — though not spiritually, for there was an ordered harmony in the unified will which no amount of activity could have shaken—stretched taut. Activity and even pressure can emerge from the contemplative soul, but there is nothing to prevent these things playing fast and loose with the nervous system. The spirit was willing enough, and even calm; it was the flesh that couldn't keep it up.

From the time I first met Father Bede until a year before his death we were constantly meeting. When still at school I was able, during the holidays, to visit him while he fulfilled his preaching engagements up and down the country, either lodging with him in presbyteries and seminaries and priories or else putting up at public houses nearby. Once we spent a fortnight together in Brittany. After leaving school and before becoming a monk I saw to it that the same sort of arrangement continued: we would wire our movements and bring down Bradshaw to assist. It was thus that I came to see him in many different settings and under conditions of both work and recreation. Travelling together (and heaven knows, one gets to know a person that way), sightseeing together, meeting at the houses of friends, sharing strange meals at the side of the road and in farms, drifting downstream in a punt at Oxford, and, later, searching into the same problems of the spiritual life, we came to know each other better than most men between whose ages there is the difference of some twenty years. Indeed it was everyone's experience that the barrier of years seemed non-existent: he was not of years, not of an age like other men.

My most vivid memories of those days are connected with a pleasure which he delighted in and one of the few which he allowed himself — the pleasure of swimming. There were bathes in the river at Oxford, in the Petre at Downside, on the Brittany coast, in streams and lakes both in England and abroad. The tonic effect of cold water seemed to give him a quite new vigour; swimming was to him a re-creation in a real sense, it generated energy. Perhaps it was this as much as the pleasurable aspect of a bathe that always attracted him to water. Certainly he would drag me off in all weathers with a towel, and sometimes without a towel, to one or other of those patches on the map which are marked, significantly, in blue.

Holiness, however fundamental in a character, is always from the biographer's point of view a more elusive quality than any other, and so if in these pages I am painting a picture of a dripping figure in a bathing suit it is not because I have forgotten him at the altar in a chasuble. It is simply that I see him with equal clearness on the water's edge and saying Mass. It is in the nature of this kind of painting to record what we see and not what we guess at. I know what he was like when he bathed, I can only guess at what he was like when he prayed.

Father Bede's reticence about his prayer is still a matter of surprise to me. Well as we knew each other he never — except to say that Abbot Chapman's articles were not much help to him — told me anything about his prayer. Often by talking myself about the subject of prayer in general, I tried to draw him out about his own interior life, but it was always without success. The most he would do, and this only in the last meetings which we had, was to discuss the principles of the thing in the abstract. These meetings, the last of a long series, belong to a week which I spent at Blackfriars where he was then superior. It was during August, and for an hour in the mornings and two hours in the afternoons we would sit in the sun and talk. He, which was unusual for him, did most of the talking, and I remember feeling at the time that I must lose none of it. He spoke mostly of human affection and of marriage and of the ideals that youth must follow if Christian civilisation was to survive. What he told me in that garden at Oxford I came later to regard as his testament, and it is to those leisured unstudied discussions that I owe much that has been written in this book. (Much especially that deals with Christian love is an echo of those August mornings, while the section describing leadership has Father Bede of course as model.)

He died the following year. From the first introduction twenty-five years ago my hero-worship has lost nothing of its enthusiasm; in fact my admiration has deepened as I have seen further into the nature of men. He is, I say it to my dishonour, the only one among those to whom I have been greatly attached whom I have not wanted to monopolise for myself.

This is in itself a tribute to his peculiar genius and the magic of his friendship. The same instinct which made me at the age of fifteen want to show him to my friends, to display him as something quite different from what I and my lot had so far come across, to give everyone the benefit of his charm and rope in a gang of admirers, now, twenty-five years later, makes me want to do the same. This accounts for a memoir in the middle of a quite different kind of book. Even the effort of memory which has gone into the writing of these pages, slight though they are, has revived that tingling sense of freshness which Father Bede brought to life and which we call youth. I can, considering that they have not had this man to go to, forgive the young people of this generation almost anything. We were lucky: in our day we at least had someone to whom we could take difficulties, with whom we could feel absolutely at home. We knew that our difficulties had been difficulties to him — perhaps were still. We knew that there was no question of shocking him, of being despised by him. He believed in us, and we knew it. He believed in youth. He loved youth. It was a principle with him that love, far from being blind, was the only power which could really see: it could see the lovable. This is what is meant by living with your eyes open: you see the lovable even in the unlovely. There is much in youth which is not always lovely, but to those who are near to God youth is always lovable. It was the potentiality in youth which appealed to Father Bede.

It was youth — his own as much as other people's, for he was always young — which gave him colour when all around him had gone grey. It was to youth that he gave his dwindling strength, and perhaps of all his works the most enduring will be that which he did in the service of the young. "What's the trouble now? Or have you just come to talk and be gay?" Youth asked much of Father Bede — drawing it out of him from every separate part of a many-sided nature — and received on that account nothing but what was his splendid best to give.

THE MASS

"DOES HE STILL GO TO MASS?" is asked of the Catholic who is seen to be slowing down. "Tell him about the Mass, and see what he makes of it," is said of the possible convert. "Can they get to Mass?" we wonder anxiously about people who have moved to some remote place on the map. Always it is the Mass. We are brought up with the knowledge that it is the Mass that matters, and it is this that we try and hand down to those who come after us. "As long as you stick to your weekly Mass, and Holy Communion when you can manage it," we say to the young man leaving school, "you won't go far wrong."

Then appear the stumbling blocks. Young men who go to Mass every Sunday *do* go far wrong. Young women who come over to England from Catholic countries, where apparently they have been to Mass every day of their lives, don't go near a church until the day when they set foot again upon their native shore. Whole slices of a Mass-going population are found to drop off at the first lick of persecution. How does it happen? How did Henry VIII, with his three Masses a day, come to such a bad end?

Surely the reason why the Mass doesn't always have the effect which it should and could have is because it is looked at only and not lived. "Learn of me," says our Lord from the altar, and all we do is to sit there and watch. For as long as the Mass remains for us a duty to be got through, a half-hour in church, an appointment which on pain of mortal sin we cannot afford to miss, we shall never fully benefit from it, or indeed quite realise what it is about. The Mass is not the priest's private prayer which the faithful have to attend once a week so as to maintain their Catholic status. Of course we know well enough that it is not this, we know that it is the Crucifixion over again, that it is the prayer of Christ in which we are privileged to take part, that its merit is infinite, and that it is the most perfect prayer-expression that can be offered. We know all this, but unless the knowledge is effective there is not much point in our possessing it. If the Mass is not a principle of action, a force in the regulation of life, a clue to the meaning of what Christ came on earth to teach, its significance is very largely missed. Some might hold that the stumbling blocks above referred to could be accounted for by the fact that the Mass had never been properly attended to, that those who had subsequently lapsed had never really assisted at the Mass as they should have done, that they had never followed what was going on. This may well be true, in fact must be true, but the question is how should they have followed — with a book? Surely the Mass is the centre of liturgical worship because it is Christ's sacrifice, and not, primarily, because it embodies the Church's finest prayers. Even if we miss the Church's finest prayers, and yet in our assisting at Mass are imbued with the idea of its sacrifice, we are at least grasping the essential. For the faithful to feel that they are missing a vital element of the Mass when they are unable to catch up with the prayers which are being said is to mistake the emphasis. They are asked to follow, not to catch up; to follow with their minds and hearts first, then if possible with their lips. It is doubtful whether any but an instructed Hebrew would have been able to catch up with what was performed and prayed at the Last Supper, and certainly not all who called themselves our Lord's disciples would have been able to follow, let alone catch up with, the events which culminated in the Sacrifice of Calvary.

It is the sacrifice that is the most important part; it is this and not the words in which it is couched that is the fullest expression of love. Always at the heart of man's homage to God has been this idea of sacrifice. It has been made the test of the dispositions of man. Cain and Abel were divided on their attitude towards sacrifice; the good and bad thief likewise; good and bad Catholics, perhaps, the same.

If the Catholic, then, is to question himself upon his hearing of Mass, the enquiry should be conducted on the lines of "Am I in tune with the Victim of this sacrifice?" rather than "Ought I to use a missal or can I go on saying the rosary?" If Catholics were to *live* the Mass for that short half hour, entering into the mind of the Church and the priest and the Subject of the sacrifice, the effects of it would continue throughout the day, and not limit themselves to the time of Mass itself. (I am speaking here of the effects as influencing human thought and conduct, and not from the point of view of what effect a well heard Mass may have in heaven.) Inevitable, surely, that having entered into the mind of Christ at such a time as this, the Catholic comes away more ready himself to offer, to give, to suffer. Having seen whom Christ is praying for, he sees his own place in the fellowship of Christ's Mystical Body. Appreciating the subjection and dependence which Christ imposed upon Himself with regard to man, he too is prepared to be at man's disposal all day long. By thus dwelling in the Mass and with the Mass, a habit of mind is acquired to which the more obvious selfishnesses are repugnant. From the corporal no less than from the Cross, and to most people perhaps more intimately, Christ challenges our generosity. Accepting the handling of life as the Host accepts the handling of the priest, the true Mass-Catholic rises above the disappointments which normally wreck the happiness of men. In the Mass is indeed the lesson of Christ's death, but it is the lesson of His life as well. In it we read, reflected, the purpose of our own.

THE MASS AND MARRIAGE

BETWEEN THE PREPARATION AND the consummation of the first Mass, our Lord gave to man the discourse of the Vine. The stem was just about to be severed. The grapes were to be torn away, scattered, trodden into the earth. But not all. Later, branches would shoot up from the same root, and new fruit would appear. And the fruit would remain. There would be pruning, there would be splitting, there would be the growth of strange twisted shapes. But the Vine would stand, and the grapes would go on coming year after year... The Mass and marriage.

"I am the vine, you are the branches. He that abideth in me and I in him, the same beareth much fruit. For without me you can do nothing." We have seen when treating of the Mass the necessity of reproducing the sacrificial mind of Christ; when treating of marriage we have seen the necessity of interpreting human love in terms of the love of God. With the Mass and with marriage the secret lies in abiding with Him while He abides in us.

Our Lord says "abide" in me (in the Knox translation it is "live on" in me), which means that the relationship must be a settled thing and not merely a refuge in an emergency. The Word which is made flesh *dwells* among us, and is no casual caller. Our devotion at Mass may vary because the mind is an unstable faculty, but if our wills are fixed on *abiding* in Christ we have there a foundation, an anchorage: we *are in* Christ. The relationship is established. And in the case of that other relationship, the union between man and wife, here too if the wills of both members are turned towards Christ the fruit of the sacrament is guaranteed, "As the branch cannot bear fruit of itself unless it abide in the vine, so neither can you unless you abide in me." A Catholic can't make a success of his marriage unless he abides in Christ. Where will the fruit come from if he is not a branch of the vine? From self presumably. This is no fruit at all. "Every branch that beareth not fruit He will take away." Without Him, Christ tells us again, we can do nothing. Yet we seem to do so much. We are always doing things. How many of them are done "in Him"? To take only the two which we are considering: the Mass can't be anything without Christ, and certainly marriage can't be much. A branch without reference to the vine. Tear away a branch and you can't make it live for long — not for longer than the leaves remain on it. "Without me you can do nothing": nothing that lasts, nothing that has any value. Whatever we achieve on our own steam serves only our own steam: it is a vapour. A purity which is designed to keep a man fit is no fruit of the vine; an attendance at Mass which aims at preserving the tradition of a name is no fruit of the vine. The branch cannot bear fruit of itself: its so-called fruits are what Maurice Baring calls *pêches à quinze sous* — they look very nice in the basket, but then you see others a little further on which are marked *à trente sous* and you see the difference. "He shall be cast forth as a branch and he shall wither." Not all at once perhaps, but eventually. His generosity will become display, his tolerance will become a condoning of evil, his tenderness will become soft.

In the Mass — which is to say in Christ — is to be found the clue to the married life. The offering of two souls and bodies finds perfect precedent in the offering of Christ's soul and body. It is the altar of love in either case. The very symbolism of the Mass is suited: as the ears of wheat are mingled in the making of the host and as the cluster of grapes becomes one thing in the formation of the wine, so the two become one in the sacrament of marriage. The resources are pooled, independence is renounced, the contribution is so united that what each brings is indistinguishable from the other and can never again revert to its own unwedded identity. Together the two members of the partnership give to each other and to God in the way that Christ gives to mankind and to the Father in the Mass. Sacrifice is the key. Almost intolerable at times must seem the burden of the married state. But then this is what one would expect of a life which Christ has dignified with the gift of a sacrament. A burden? But for those who take up their cross and follow Christ the burden —He promises it—is light. The yoke—even that yoke to which two souls harness themselves so hopefully on the morning of their wedding and which is perhaps only fully understood in later years—is sweet. But the condition stands: "You in me, and I in you."

THE CHALLENGE

THE PART OF THE REFORMER is a very difficult one to play. It is so easy to overplay it. Zeal has a way of stampeding us into the world of the faintly ridiculous, and the possible good that we could be doing is wasted. In endeavouring to put right an abuse we must be careful not to abuse our endeavour. Exaggerate the correction, and the corrected will exaggerate the exaggeration. People who are pounced upon with disproportionate energy are inclined to laugh at those who are correcting them, and so will minimise the faults that have been singled out for correction. Thus if the restraining influence is to be of any use it must itself be more restrained than the influence which it aims at restraining. If you want to cure a man of swearing, you don't do it by the violence of your language; if you want to stop two children fighting, you don't rush in and knock them both down. The distinction between righteous indignation and the common or garden kind will not be appreciated: for the lesson to sink in with any fullness there is need for contrast between your behaviour and the behaviour which you want reformed. The above are hypothetical examples; let me give a concrete instance. Once when I was young, an undergraduate friend of mine with whom I was travelling happened to throw a quantity of lightly made cheese soufflé at an electric fan in the first-class dining saloon of a P. & O. liner. The third of our party, a don, said in a dry, flat (but not sarcastic) voice and without looking up from his plate: "I wish you wouldn't do that; it only upsets people." We had little in common, this don and I, and indeed my taste was then rather in favour of mild disturbances in public places, but I know that at that moment I could have followed him to the world's end and would have cheerfully cut myself to pieces in his service. My contemporary must have felt much the same, for he assures me that from that day to this he has never, under whatever provocation, thrown a single soufflé into the whirling blades of an electric fan.

There may be times when correction is more telling if directed with vehemence, and there may be people whom only the more forceful measures will convince. Our Lord, after all, cast out the money changers with violence from the Temple. But this was a single occasion, and the money changers were singularly hard cases. Even with the Pharisees who, if anyone ever did, deserved what they got, our Lord's dealings were measured. It was the challenge of His restraint which converted souls, not the sting of His reproof. With the woman taken in adultery, with the Samaritan woman, with Judas himself, our Lord showed the force of under- rather than over-emphasis on guilt. Some rose to meet the challenge, others didn't. It was a challenge, moreover, that he wanted to see thrown out by those who followed Him. James and John, He said, were not restrained enough. Peter in

Gethsemani was also too violent. That was not the way to make converts. The sword had to be put back in the scabbard; the twelve legions of angels which could have been summoned at any moment to His aid would not be wanted; the Son of Man had not come to destroy.

Before the High Priest, before Herod, before Pilate, before the world, Christ could have justified Himself. But He chose to remain silent. He could have reviled but He did not revile. As a lamb that is led to the slaughter, so did Christ allow Himself to be led ... and He opened not His mouth. Again a challenge. In the face of this, you either respond or you fight; you cannot say "how very interesting" and leave it at that. Noise can be challenging as well as silence, but there comes a point when noise deafens you and you no longer hear its challenge. Silence is much more of a challenge because you are mystified by it, you feel uncomfortable, it searches you much more closely than noise. You have to go on and find an answer. "But Jesus held His peace and answered not a word." It defeated them utterly.

Silence speaks of a strength which can only be guessed at, a reserve which may be drawn upon at any moment. The force which is suggested but not revealed is often a more compelling influence than the force which appears. It is an impressive sight to watch a man whom you know to have a powerful temper restraining himself. It is more exciting to see him letting himself go, but you are more impressed if he doesn't. After a stormy meeting: "Why didn't you lash out? You could have flattened them." "It wouldn't have done." Impressive. A challenge.

No less in art and literature and sport is this the case, and certainly is this so in dealing with souls. There must always be a margin of unrevealed potentiality, whether it is of talent or of virtue or of physical endurance. Otherwise the stock is seen to be exhausted. Where there is no further room for expectation there is also no room for confidence, or what we prefer to regard as faith. Belief in something yet to come is the answer given by one soul to another. If there is nothing more to come, it means there has been no restraint. The challenge has been taken up in vain. Because it could never have been justified, it should never have been made. There was no reserve.

Not only is the restraint which we exercise a challenge to others, calling upon their generosity and their faith, but it is a challenge also to our own capacity: can we operate it positively, or is it merely a security wall behind which is marshalled our potential? Put quite simply, can we be patient when we want to rush through our reforms? Can we be gentle when we feel like being harsh? Can we smooth the way for souls, or must we plough up the ground and send them running along the furrows? This gets us back to the beginning, where we considered the danger of exaggeration and the zeal which all too easily stampedes. Let us be on our guard lest in the reclaiming of a single soul made after the image and likeness of God Himself we fumble clumsily and spoil the work. There must be no rough handling here.

If the intemperate apostleship of a Jehu does damage to souls instead of good, so also does that other quest for souls which brings them back to self and not to God. To many — there are some who would say to all — there comes at least once in a lifetime the chance of re-making a soul that has been broken up to bits. The process may be one of gradual rebuilding, or (more rarely) of dramatic and rapid transformation. Whichever it is, it is a work and not a magic. It is a work done under the power of grace or it is no work of God at all. It is a work which has come from God and must go back to God. It has to do with a soul which has come from God and must go back to God. God offers us the chance of joining with Him in His act of re-creating a soul. An offer? Yes, and more — a challenge. Say we take up this challenge and work with Him. Say we win over the soul whom Providence has marked out as ours to give to God. Say we are not detached enough, restrained enough; say we begin to look upon that soul as a gift to us which we deserve and not as a gift to God which He has given us the grace to win; say we appropriate what is His; say we forget that He could have worked without us all along, and but for His restraint could have taken the work out of our hands at any moment . . . just as He could at any moment have sent for those twelve legions of angels and stopped the Passion. . . . Is not restraint, every way you look at it, a challenge?

APPROACH TO MYSTICISM

CHRISTIAN MYSTICISM IS NOT a thing apart, a sort of added faculty or sixth sense, a miraculous charisma which anyone else, or you yourself for that matter, can detect at once. "This man has mysticism...that one has not." No. Certainly it is, in the theological and philosophical sense, a habit—it is part of the habit of religion—but it is not the kind you can always put your finger on. There may be some whom one would call mystics straight away, but the vast majority of mystics are those who, though they possess the habit, enjoy the awareness of it so rarely (if at all) and experience its activity so intermittently and secretly that, even if they themselves know of what is going on inside them, we others outside could easily pass them over in a crowd or in a community without ever noticing anything mystical about them.

All that Christian mysticism amounts to is union with God, or—if you like to look at it from the way in which it reveals itself—the development of the Christ-life within the soul. So it stands to reason that outwardly there may be very little to show for this. Who—apart from the obvious cases among the saints—is a mystic and who isn't? In heaven there is no doubt about it: everyone is a mystic. But on earth God alone can know. On earth few souls are habitually united to God in the highest mystical sense, and even in the widest sense of being united to Him in the possession of sanctifying grace it is not all the world who can lay the claim. The ordinary Catholic who is not in mortal sin is united to God, but he is not a mystic. He is, however, a potential mystic. If God wants him to be one and if he co-operates, he has all the material there — in the sacraments and sanctifying grace. The closest union, however, is necessarily for the few. But even in saying this there is the misleading suggestion that the soul has to climb on to a particular kind of pedestal which is measured to a specific height. A better way of looking at it would be to discard the idea of the soul mounting to union, as it were step by step until a certain altitude is reached, and to think of it as the soul becoming increasingly united in all its operations. Exterior operations as well as interior. God becomes more and more the setting in which everything is lived. And more than the setting even; He becomes the life itself. "For to me to live is Christ" says St. Paul.

St. Gertrude says that the indwelling of grace is a fact of which her contemplation has given her deeper and deeper knowledge. Her experience is common; it is a knowledge which souls who give themselves to prayer normally arrive at. It is, under God of course, the logical consequence. This indwelling of the Spirit is the subject of most of Père Plus's writing, and indeed it is a theme which is receiving more attention today from spiritual writers than ever before. The expansion of the Christ-life, its gradual unfolding and assimilation, is the essence of Christian mysticism. But since Baptism the Christ-life has been there all along. Mysticism, in germ, has been there all along. Though present, however, this life of the Spirit within has been known only in the same sort of way that what is going on in one's hands and feet is known. We appreciate without thinking that there is life in our hands and feet, but it doesn't seem to matter much. When we think of life we think of something closer. Until we think of it as something closer we might just as well *be* a hand or a foot. With the mystic the understanding of life is more close and more real and more comprehensive than with the ordinary person. The mystic life is not a hand or foot life. The mystic is right on top of the life stream, and can see what the whole organism is about. His vision is clearer than ours; not different but more direct. It is the Christ-life shining through. It is the single eye of which our Lord speaks in the Sermon on the Mount, which causes the whole body to be lightsome.

MYSTICISM IN OPERATION

AFTER CONSIDERING THE nature of the mystic element in a person's life the next question is to examine its effects. We have decided that the mystic habit itself need not draw attention to the mystic; there is no real reason why its effects should either. If they do, they are the accidental rather than the essential effects. The essential effects are far too subtle to be seen. Even the director, unless he is more than usually skilled, and unless the accounts he receives of the soul's progress are more than usually revealing, will find it none too easy to judge of what is really going on in the inner life of the soul that is in the mystic way.

Viewing life more simply, the growing mystic will tend to behave more simply; but that from the outside is about all that will show for it. Looking at the world from a bird's-eye view he will tend to be somewhat in the clouds, but this is a symptom which naturally follows the application to most branches of thought and need not be taken as proper to mysticism. Also it is not by any means always present. St. Teresa was not a dreamy person, and there was nothing vague or wafting about St. Benedict or St. Gregory or St. Bernard. Where such signs are evident, as in the cases of Blessed John Ruysbroeck and St. Joseph Cupertino for instance, they are no more than the consequence of their absorption in God. Absorption in God need not produce these effects, but it very often does. Absorption in any thought process, even if it's only preparing a speech or composing a limerick, very often does. As with the speculative mathematician and the creative artist, so often with the mystic: the closer he gets to his particular facet of Truth, the more of his time, as well as the more of his energy, is taken up in dwelling upon the object of his search. Whether or not absent-mindedness ensues in the case of the mystic, certainly recollection does, and this is one of the effects which we have in mind when we talk of mysticism in operation.

Recollection? The term covers a good deal, but it would be a mistake to think of it as meaning an habitual awareness of God's presence or of spiritual truths. We can be more or less recollected all day long, but we can hardly be thinking of spiritual things all day long. Surely recollection means being ordered in our lives within, and unified in our activity without. The more a man becomes a mystic the more ordered he is inside, and the more he tends to see things outside himself as a unity. All is in God's purpose and God's purpose is in all. The mystic is not a mystic because he prays while he is shaving or while he is waiting to get through on the telephone; he is a mystic because he is so united to God by the grace which is in him as a continually developing force that he sees everything in terms of the supernatural rather than the natural. The spiritual is more real, more alive to him, than the physical. To him there is no point in worrying about his life, what he shall eat, about his body, what he shall put on; he knows that if the grass of the field which is today, and tomorrow is cast into the oven, God doth so clothe, then he and all his cares are well provided for. Obviously, then, if the created order has meaning to the mystic only in so far as it is seen to reflect the divine, recollection (in the sense that we have described it) becomes almost habitual. So he probably *will* pray while he shaves and telephones; though it is not this, as I have suggested, that qualifies him as a mystic.

Again, and arising out of the above, an effect of the mystic habit is to transcend the divisions into which life and all its activities normally fall. This is not to claim that the mystic man may either behave or think in an arbitrary way (though it must be admitted that some mystics do); it is to suggest that the mystic's outlook is such that life, and particularly the spiritual life, is not so much a passing from one activity to another, a series of happenings in time, as a single activity which expresses itself uniformly in various different works. The expression is uniform because the direction is Godward. Everything in the mystic's life has the same object. Everything has the same interpretation. Everything is kept together by the same unifying principle. Thus to the mystic his own happiness and his own holiness are not two things, but one. His work is not a separate thing which he will do well if he is happy and holy and gets God to help him; his work is part and parcel of both his happiness and his holiness. To look upon our occupations as things which we must influence by our personal goodness *as it were from on top* is to give a false orientation. Better than saying: "I must take care to do my best spiritually or else this activity of mine will be a failure," is to say: "The will of God which is in this work must, if I let it, bring the best out of me spiritually." Holiness, surely, *follows* the will of God; it doesn't precede it. The same applies to happiness: we seek first the kingdom of God, and then we turn round to find that both these things have been added. There would be no need to plan out ways of sanctifying our work if we allowed our work to shape and sanctify us. The real mystics find mysticism in their work because they find both God in their work and their work in God. It is a mistake to go looking for the kind of works which have a mystic flavour in the hope that by performing them we may ourselves become mystics. Not only is the order wrong, but it is again to split up and divide where there should be unity. The way to union with God (which is what we decided was the definition of mysticism) is through union with His will. We can never be united to His will if we follow our own and choose other works than His. It is as if Christ were asking: "Do you want to know who the real mystics are? Do you want to know who is my mother and who are my brethren? I'll tell you. Behold the real mystics, behold my mother and my brethren . . . whosoever shall do the will of my Father that is in heaven, he is my brother and sister and mother."

THE MYSTIC'S CHARITY

MISTAKENLY WE THINK of the mystic as being so caught up in the contemplation of divine things that there is little room for acts of human charity. His prayer for the world at large, we say, excuses him from the service of his neighbour; he can't be expected to come down to the love of man if he is always occupied with the love of God. It is nice of us to defend the mystic like this but of course there is no need; we are entirely wrong. The mystic loves man more, not less, in virtue of his mysticism; his service must if anything be wider than the ordinary man's because with clearer perception all are seen to be his neighbour; his active ministry is proportioned to his contemplative call; he works for man *ex abundantia contemplationis*, and there is *abundantia* about his labour of love for man.

If there is anything aloof and distant about the man whom we suspect of being a mystic, then we have reason to think that there may be something not quite genuine about his mysticism. At all events it is not in virtue of his mysticism that he stands away from his fellow men; it is probably in virtue of his natural habit which has not yet been subdued to the influence of grace. Grace is expansive; it is self that contracts and works its way inwards. *Bonitas est diffusiva sui*, and if there is no *diffusiva* there is no true *bonitas*. The withdrawal from the world and from unnecessary activity which accompanies the contemplative vocation is no withdrawal from charity, it is merely the avoidance of all that would endanger the soul's recollection as understood in the terms of the foregoing essay. The ordered unity must be preserved at all cost, and anything from without that threatens to disturb its foundations must be kept at arm's length. This is no mere running away from petty distraction, no question either of avoiding responsibility, no top-soil dressing that is being preserved; it is a question here of safeguarding the essential quality of the life. Withdrawal on these lines is no neglect of charity; in fact charity would not be preserved if there were no withdrawal. If the mystic or the contemplative were to sacrifice his ordered unity within, he would find that he was sacrificing at the same time his active charity without. The first thing to happen would be the break-up of his love for man, the tarnishing of his charity. He would be finding self where before he found others, he would be loving individuals wrongly where before he loved all men rightly. The whole point of the mystic vision, as we have suggested, is that it sees everything as a unity, everything integrated. If this goes, all else goes. The danger is that charity may be made an excuse for losing charity. God is love, and He must not be divided against himself. Charity is a coat without seam. "To those that love God, all things work together for good." All things. Nothing then, and least of all the duty of charity towards one's neighbour, may be left out. Mysticism doesn't leave it out, it puts it in its proper place: it sees it in relation to the rest, as part of the unified whole. If the mystic is simply the man whose whole being is supernaturalised — whose work, whose happiness, whose external contacts, whose sufferings are found on a spiritual level — then obviously what he does for souls will fit in. It is not only "for them do I sanctify myself," but "*through* them do I sanctify myself." Souls are, rightly ordered as they take their place in my life, the means to my sanctification. There is no distraction here, no pull away from God. The mystic is able to give so much to souls precisely because he has given so much to God. It is the effect of the Christ-life developing within him that none who cross his horizon are thought undeserving of his charity. Nothing escapes his goodwill and everything ministers to his goodness. There is a Persian proverb which says: "Help thou thy brother's boat across, and lo! thine own has touched the shore." As long as our own boat is the main preoccupation we can never hope to be true mystics. Long for the shore, yes, but long still more for the glory of God . . . and it is certain that He is glorified in the execution of His Commandment. The service of God and the service of man run parallel, they are one in principle. Fulfil the conditions of this service, and the development of sanctity together with the discovery of happiness can be left to God; they follow naturally, they overflow. It is the mystic who sees this and acts upon it. Anyone can see it and act upon it. But how few do. Need we wonder that there are so few finished mystics? Or that among those who are, there is little to show outwardly for their mysticism? The programme sounds so easy; perhaps it is the execution that is, even to the mystic, so difficult. At any rate it is the whole and only secret of the mystic approach. It is faith, hope and charity; that is why.

APPROACH TO ASCETICISM

"OH LORD," THE NEOPHYTE might groan at this point, "not content with wanting us to be mystics, he wants us to be ascetics as well; it's a little hard." No one is asked to be either a mystic or an ascetic; it is simply that fidelity to an unrestricted way of grace normally leads to these things, and it is such a fidelity that is inculcated in the pages of this book. Also it would be a mistake to think that the matter divided itself neatly into departments: one for the mystics and one for the ascetics. "Choose which you like . . . or both." No. It is a question, again, of unity and not of separation. Mysticism and asceticism are each expressions of the same thing, aspects of the same thing. Love is the principle revealing itself in either form, but both forms are so inter-related as to perform the same work. It is the candle of love burning away merrily at both ends.

Just as mysticism was seen to be the unfolding of the Christ-life, so is asceticism seen to be exactly the same thing. Just as mystics may be regarded as the extensions of Christ living, so ascetics may be regarded as the extensions of Christ dying. Always Christ as the centre and source of either activity. And because Christ is one, the follower of Christ must be one. Because Christ lived and suffered, the follower must live and suffer. Nothing of the Christ-life may be left out. Every soul, however distantly he walks in the footsteps of Christ, must have something of the mystic in him and something of the ascetic. Prayer and penance of *some* sort have got to find a place in the life of every Christian. The duties of Catholicism may be lightly borne, but there isn't a member of the Church who would claim that he could dispense with worship and self-denial. Not only are both commanded by Christ and by the Church, but — and it is this aspect of it that is more to the present purpose — they are both necessitated by the development of grace within the soul. The indwelling spirit is the leaven which our Lord speaks about as the Kingdom of Heaven: it spreads until the whole being is leavened. Everything is expanded under its influence, nothing escapes. Penance, as part of the whole which goes up from the soul to God, is thus leavened together with the rest. Penance, as part of the debt which is paid by man to God, is thus caught up in the sweep of grace. Duty is transformed and made a prayer, the debt is transformed and made an act of praise.

The error in asceticism, no less than in mysticism, is to approach the idea from the wrong end. We tend to look upon penance almost exclusively as being that collection of practices which we have to go in for if we are to satisfy our obligation towards this particular demand of our religion. Admittedly we are rather forced by practical considerations to come upon the question of penance from this angle. We have to say "What shall I give up for Lent?" "I am smoking too much, I must cut it down." Circumstances oblige us, in other words, to think of penance in terms of measures to adopt, rather than in terms of sufferings to allow. But the more we can get into the way of seeing it as a chance sent to us by God, as a means of praising Him and not only as a means of correcting ourselves, as part of our prayer and not as something to be screwed on from outside, as the necessary expression of the Christ-life within rather than as an arbitrary expression of self-life without, the better. We have a perfect illustration of the rightly ordered approach to penance in our Lord's own simile, the vine. The main consideration should not be to bring our own gardener devices to the tending of the branches, each branch being separate and having a different direction from the rest, but much more to allow the sap all possible freedom in coming up the parent stem and extending to the farthest twig.

Just as we saw in mysticism the tendency of man towards multiplicity, so we see the same in asceticism. It is only the true mystic and the true ascetic — by which is meant the saint — who so sees life as a unity that there is no divorce between the natural and the supernatural order, no division between the mystical and ascetical element. The saint sees Christ so clearly in the Church that there is nothing extraordinary about being martyred for the Church; he sees Christ so clearly in the leper that there is nothing extraordinary about kissing the sores of the leper; he sees so much more than we do in the Mass, in the liturgy, in human love, in joy and suffering and hard work, that there is never anything extraordinary in the actions which these things inspire. It is the ordinary and not the extraordinary thing for the saint to show love for his enemy, to spend hours with people who try him, to do anything in the world that obedience suggests. He sees Christ in all this. It is the non-saint who sees incongruity where there should be order and consistency; it is the sinner who can't understand how the sacrament of marriage can be squared with the act of married love, how God's goodness can be squared with the suffering in His universe, how hell can be squared with our conception of Divine Mercy. To the saint these things seem perfectly in order. They *are* in order — that's exactly why. They are in the order of God's Providence which we so often miss. The saint sees Good Friday as God sees it. "If that day, of all days in the history of the world, was good," argues the saint, "then suffering which is naturally an evil can be supernaturally a good . . . in which case the more I have of it the better." And he accepts the call to asceticism. To live is Christ, says St. Paul, and the Christ whom he knows and preaches is Christ crucified. Here is the only approach to Christian asceticism: through Christ re-lived in the soul. When our Lord said that

He must suffer, Peter said no, that this wouldn't do. For protesting against the necessity of His having to suffer, Peter was called Satan and told that he savoured not of the things that were of God but the things that were of man — that he was using the world's voice. "He that will save his life shall lose it," said our Lord, developing His rebuke to Peter, "and he that will lose his life for my sake shall find it." So for Christians there is no mistaking the absolute necessity, in some shape, of asceticism.

ASCETICISM IN OPERATION

"YES, BUT BY WAY OF JUSTIFYing his asceticism, what does an ascetic *do*?" Practices are always more in demand than principles; we always like to get down to the human element and the concrete test; it's how the thing works out that interests us, not the motive. Statistics fascinate us, and yet they almost always mislead. In the spiritual life the favourite question is "How must I act?" when the more important one would be "How should I think?" It has always been the same: Saul on the way to Damascus opened his relationship with God by saying "What wilt thou have me to do?" Perhaps by the time he was Paul he was saying "Lord, what wilt thou have me to be?"

We think of the mystic, and at once ecstasies suggest themselves to the mind; we think of the ascetic and immediately fasts and floggings and boards in beds appear. In order to find out, however, what asceticism in operation really is we should avoid consulting a list of standard austerities and go behind all this to the study of what mysticism in operation really is. The spirit of the two, it has been decided above, is the same, and though they will express themselves differently in their separate operations they will do so along the same lines. Thus if mysticism's activity consists in allowing positively the life of grace to sanctify through life itself, asceticism's activity is allowing positively the life of grace to sanctify *through that particular part of life* which has to do with suffering. Whether voluntary or involuntary, outward or inward, sent by God or provided by man, suffering is the ground and medium of asceticism. Asceticism is another word for self-denial: there is the self in the senses which has to be denied, and the self in the will which has to be denied. Now because there is more self in the will than there is in the senses, asceticism's primary work is to be found in the will. The principle to be acted upon in the renunciation of each of these selves is suggested by what has already been discussed in a previous essay: namely whatever is found to be a menace to ordered unity must go. This scheme of renunciation works all the way up the scale from sense to spirit. First to be renounced, as disturbing the necessary balance, are occasions of sin; next imperfections, distracting influences, self-indulgences, and so on until perfectly harmless and legitimate things are renounced — not any longer because they are obstacles or even immortifications but simply because the renunciation of them is an expression of the love of God. From here the next stage is to leave self out of consideration altogether, renouncing it in the sense of forgetting it, and to bend all one's energy towards giving to God without further counting the cost. Such is asceticism in operation. There may or may not be hair-shirts and disciplines, just as there may or may not be actual prayer for most of the day in the case of the mystic, but the main thing is that the habit of asceticism is passing from diversity to unity, from the negative *agere contra* to the positive *agere pro*, from the self-conscious choice of this and that practice to the self-oblivious choice of God. The particular penances will probably be there all right — the hair-shirt and so on — but they will be taken in the general sweep towards God and not allowed to become a fascination. It is the self-giving, not particularised or canalised, that matters. It is one thing to surrender what one has and even what one wants, but it is quite another to surrender what one is.

Take, Lord, these things in sacrifice,
These people, places, hopes, and all beside.
And let me look upon the hollow in my heart
With eyes unshot with bitterness;
And if there's more Thou covetest,
Then give the grace, and I and mine shall part.

What, Lord, it's not these things Thou callest for, but me?
It is not what I love but what I am?
Then is the secret not in nakedness?
In laying waste the pastures of the heart?
Speak, Lord, and tell me what I yet can give
Beyond the yielding of my heart's desires.

"It's time to be, O Soul, not now to die;
Surrender what you are, not what you own.
Aim at no form, no state, no measure of your love.
Leave self aside and search for Me alone."

True asceticism has self-abandonment as its strong suit—ultimately as its only suit. Again is this for no other reason than because its way and the way of mysticism run parallel. Abandonment to the indwelling of the Spirit, to the unqualified operation of grace, to the free development of the Christ-life within the soul.

THE ASCETIC'S CHARITY

IF THE MYSTIC'S CHARITY IS suspected of being cold, the ascetic's charity is similarly presumed to be harsh. "He has declared war on the flesh...which probably includes all flesh, not merely his own." Where the mystic is accused of pursuing the supernatural to the neglect of the natural, the ascetic is accused of pursuing the harder until he ceases to sympathise with the easier. This is a misconception; the ascetic, if he is on the right lines, is the mildest and kindest and most tolerant of men. Should his penances make him savage it is a sign that they must be dropped. His austerities are the evidence of his charity, not of his uncharity; they reflect what is going on within. The only excuse for the fierceness of his self-denial is the heat of his love: love for God and love for man. If there is any other motive than that of charity, his mortifications might just as well not be practised at all; in fact they are doing him harm. The penance that doesn't result in God's glory results in vain glory, so we do well to get the direction of this matter right. The ascetic is a man of prayer and a man of charity, or else he is, at best, an eccentric. In the last analysis we judge these principles by the people who profess them, and nowhere will you find such charity as among the Carthusians. They are ascetics if any are; Parkminster positively tingles with the warmth of fraternal charity.

The ascetic finds his inspiration in his prayer and not in the thought of toughness. Being hard with himself is only the logical consequence of living close to the life of Christ: for him to choose the soft way when Christ chose the hard is not to be thought of for a moment. When, in his *Seven Pillars*, Lawrence prayed

> *Lord, I was free of all Thy flowers*
> *But I chose the world's sad roses,*
> *And that is why my feet are torn*
> *And mine eyes are blind with sweat,*

Let us hope that his feet had been treading the way to Calvary, and that the sweat bore conscious relation to the Agony. Positive, united to Christ's pains, outgoing from self is the suffering of the ascetic. Just in so far as he is united to Christ is he able, therefore, to express his urge for mortification in a way that doesn't interfere with charity. How then can he, if he is yoked to the yoke of Christ, be critical of those who do not practise what he practises? How can he be dismissive in his manner, ruthless in his advice, rigid in his interpretation? Suffering with Christ, he sees with Christ, and so, with Christ, loves man.

"Yes," you say, "but it must be with a chill sort of emotion nevertheless. It can't be otherwise. Has not the ascetic renounced his attachment to creatures?

In giving up himself, has he not already given up his earthly affections? His love may embrace the universe, but it certainly seems to rule out any idea of personal response. The ascetic's love is a forced thing of the deliberating will and not at all the spontaneous sentiment which we call love."

The difficulty is a real one. That it can be met we have proof in our Lord's words: "Everyone that hath left house or brethren or sisters or father or mother or lands for my name's sake shall receive a hundredfold, and shall possess life everlasting." This must mean that the soul separates itself, as it thinks permanently, from creatures and the love of creatures, only to find that its sacrifice has been the same as Abraham's all along, and that the creatures are given back again. Not only are they given back, but the joy of their possession is increased a hundred times over, and everyone lives happily ever afterwards. How does this come about? Is it due to the whole-hearted quality of the renunciation? What is the secret of this apparent paradox whereby the soul that strips itself of everything suddenly finds itself richer than anybody else?

The solution would appear to be in the principle which has already received so much attention in these pages: namely the interaction between mysticism and asceticism. In the progress of prayer and the spiritual life an attitude of mind has grown up which sees creatures in their proper perspective. Together with the initial renunciation and fidelity to that renunciation which the call to the interior life involved, there has been a corresponding development of recollection. With the result that whatever was enjoyed inordinately at first is now, after the interval of training and separation, enjoyed rightly. And because enjoyed rightly, enjoyed more. Unruly affections are unruly no longer; attachments are all the more satisfying by reason of the detachment with which they are possessed; pleasures which used to be distracting are now a help rather than a hindrance. Creatures have taken their proper place in the scheme of things, they are seen in perspective, they are taken in the soul's sweep for what they are worth, they are understood at last as terms and symbols in the promulgated decrees of God.

Elsewhere (in *Watch and Pray*) I have suggested the simile of a boatman pushing off from the shore: as he separates himself from familiar landmarks he becomes so enveloped in a mist as to be able to distinguish nothing; then, when the mist has served its purpose, he begins to see things again; but not as they were when he dwelt among them on land; he sees them now as emerging from the mist. The ascetic, because he is necessarily part mystic, sees creatures in God. Hitherto he made it his business to see God in creatures wherever possible, now wherever he looks he sees them in God. Far from toning down his love for God's created order this new vision adds to its colour and its life. Less selfishly are the lovely things of this world loved, but not less loved. If we shrink from the starkness of the ascetic's approach we have only to remember that on our Lord's authority the grain of wheat must die first before it can really begin to live. So our too earthly love must die before it can be said to live. To our ungenerous and shortsighted minds there is the dread of shedding anything of our love — even if the part of it that we have to shed lies wholly in the senses and is precious little use to us at any time — when really we should value the chance of being led, through sacrifice, to the experience of a truer love. It is not through a frosted glass that the ascetic looks on life, but rather through the eyes of God. He sees and understands, and therefore loves.

With the ascetic, then, no less than with the mystic it is the law of love that gives him life. If in the individual soul the elements must, for the purposes of discussion, be divided, then it might be said that where the mystic's charity gives all to man because it has given all to God, the ascetic's charity suffers all for man because he has suffered all for God. No toughness here, no tight-lipped cult of pain; this is the asceticism which knows no greater love than that a man should lay down his life for his brethren.

SENSITIVENESS

I HAVE A FRIEND WHO COMES to me at intervals and asks me for advice. The procedure is invariably the same, so on every occasion I know exactly what is going to happen. My advice gives instant offence, and there is a scene. Two days later my friend comes along again, and this time gives me advice (for which I have not asked), and there is another scene. The same evening we are on the best of terms as usual, and so we remain until some new crisis has to be met, some new decision has to be made, when the whole thing begins all over again. I should add that we neither of us ever dream of acting upon each other's advice.

There is this paradox to be observed about touchiness, that though vulnerable to the highest degree the people who suffer from it are ringed about by the most impenetrable of walls. You can never get it home to a touchy person that he is liable to work himself into a state over absolutely nothing. He is so deeply entrenched in his position that no amount of attack that you can bring to him will be the slightest use — it will only make for further grievances — so the only thing to do is to reverse the process and bring him to the attack. A case of the mountain being brought to Mahomet — with the additional interest that in nine cases out of ten this particular mountain turns out to be a molehill. Show to a touchy person that you are every bit as touchy yourself, and with any luck he will be shamed into an examination of his conscience. There is nothing so revealing as the sight of our own faults glaringly reflected in others.

Sensitiveness is not the same as touchiness but it can become that. Both are founded on the same error, which is an exaggerated emphasis on self. But where the touchy person gets his sense of proportion wrong and worries unduly about here-and-now minutiae, the sensitive person gets his sense of proportion right but feels too acutely about life as a whole. The touchy person can be slighted but not seriously hurt, the sensitive person can be both slighted and hurt. It is an over-delicate sensibility that the sensitive person is suffering from; it is an over-estimation of his own significance that is at the bottom of the touchy person's troubles. Sensitive people are to be pitied but not encouraged; touchy people are to be neither pitied nor encouraged. Handled rightly, a sensitive nature can be brought to produce works of high virtue and real value — works which perhaps none but sensitive natures would possess the subtlety to perform — whereas from the touchy you get nothing but fitful labours and grudging, suspicious, vainglorious and spotlight service. Handled wrongly, of course, a sensitive nature can become a torture to itself and to everyone else. Sympathy, thoughtfulness, loyalty, tenderness are among the virtues of the sensitive, so it is certainly not the purpose of this essay to advocate toughness. It is only that the drawbacks attaching to petty susceptibility belong also to being thinner skinned than nature intended the human being to be, and for this reason it would be a folly to make a cult of one's delicate sensibility. The truth is that tough natures need refining, and delicate sensibilities need training. What this amounts to is that if you make too much a point of being sensitive you may well find yourself being touchy.

Monks and nuns know all about the place which both these elements can occupy in the community life. Like salt to food, the cloister seems to bring out the taste of natural qualities whether favourable or unfavourable. A sensitive soul who has come through his time of trial can be of inestimable value in a religious house: gentleness, tolerance, accessibility simply radiate from such a one. "Having known misery he knows how to compassionate the miserable," and having experienced the joy of religion he knows how to stimulate it in others. Against this you have the sensitive soul which is preoccupied with itself: everything is seen from a necessarily cramped position and viewed solely in personal terms. To such a one the life is simply what other people do to him or her, and not what he or she can do towards the life. Vocation must mean the call to rise above sense with its too personal susceptibilities, and not only above the senses with their too natural desires.

Turning from the cloister to the hearth, the possibilities of sensitiveness in marriage, both as a menace and as a good, are clearly no less great. In all human relationship, but particularly in the closeness of married life, there is need to cultivate a perception, subtle and immediate, of the other person's point of view. This is sensitiveness working properly, giving that awareness of another's wishes, fears, sorrows, doubts, temptations and so on which leads to taking steps to meet these emotions. It makes for a considerateness which anticipates outward expression or demands from the other side. It makes people in the highest degree unselfish. Sensitiveness working badly in the married life is a cloud of threatening blackness. It gives much the same account of itself as we have seen in the case of jealousy on an earlier page. Sniffing injuries everywhere, the over-sensitive husband or wife attributes wrong motives, forms wrong judgments, draws wrong conclusions, and makes the wrong decisions about almost everything. Grounds for willies are seen on every side: life becomes a touch-and-go affair which rules out the sense of security and mental spaciousness which is necessary to married life. What is wanted if two people are to get on with each other, whether in marriage or in friendship, is a certain mutual hair-trigger responsiveness to atmosphere — a receptivity of spirit — allied to, and governed by, a cool detached horse-sense which can tell one not to be a fool.

Ah, here comes the friend whom I mentioned above. As it is two days since I gave him some very good advice, he is now presumably going to tell me my faults. Of course I am the last person in the world to pretend that I'm perfect, and though there's nothing I welcome more than being told that I'm in the wrong when I *am* in the wrong, and while it's obviously everyone's duty to point out other people's mistakes when they *ask* for it, and in spite of the excellent motives which doubtless inspire these recriminations, I cannot help feeling — without the smallest resentment, but merely stating the fact as an objective fact — that for one whose failings are an open book to come and denounce *me* in these purely personal terms when every one of his charges is grossly exaggerated, is, to say the least of it, etc., etc. . . .

THE MODERN GOSPEL

IN THE CONTEMPORARY WORLD there is no longer the same conflict as there used to be between the spiritual and the material. The character of the conflict has altered. The spiritual, if it is admitted at all, is simply pushed out of the way on the grounds that the material calls for more immediate attention. The implication is that not a moment can be spared on what at best is but a metaphysical speculation. There must be no talk of absolute certainties, of fundamental belief. Material effort—whether towards conquest, prosperity, or stark survival—has priority. Attention to supernatural values is an extra—like fancy needlework. Though pledged to right reason, religion is regarded in the eyes of the world as irrational. Irrational both in its claims upon human conduct and human credulity. Which means that unreason, the truly irrational, has forced its way into the place which the world once gave to the spiritual. If the first among Christian virtues—that of loving one's enemies—has been written off as unreasonable, it won't be long before the rest will go by the board as well. "We are fighting a life and death struggle," says the world, "and we can't be expected either to trust in a strength which we don't see, or to abide by a code of conduct which our enemies don't recognise. The risk is too great. It's unreasonable."

But isn't the whole lesson of Christianity intended to show us that sometimes we have to do unreasonable things?—in order to defend reason? The Cross was a folly according to the world's kind of reason. We *have* to trust in a strength which we don't see; our strength is precisely in the code which our enemies don't recognise. "Blessed are they that have not seen but have believed." "We look not at the things which are seen, but at the things which are not seen; for the things which are seen are temporal, but the things which are not seen are eternal."

Now if traditional morality is no longer accepted as the norm, what is going to come in and take its place? How are people, when they have decided that the Gospel is no longer practical, going to guide their lives? The answer is — they aren't going to. There won't be a norm. The tragedy is that just when man most needs Christianity he is cutting himself off from it. Having claimed that to a world in anguish the Gospel idea is too far removed from reality to be of any use, man goes on being in anguish and at the same time can find no gospel of his own in which he can place the remotest trust.

It is here that the contemplative and the ascetic may be brought to the rescue. Put it this way: mankind has become, as an organism, overtaxed in one department and dangerously undernourished in another. The interior life of man has wilted. At one time, in what was a far more balanced order of civilisation, man was able to think and pray and labour at his own work. Nor was this the order which existed in Eden before the Fall; it was the ordinary state of man in simpler times. Man has been called forth from this to serve materialism. Not to serve nature as God made it, but to serve things as man makes them. Man has served materialism very well. Much too well. It is killing him. It is only the mystic who can redress the balance. By generating energy of a different kind and on a different plane, the spiritual man counters the drive towards absolute materialism. The saint is an expert in a different science altogether. It is his corresponding efficiency, his vision, his staying power which alone can arrest the course of this Frankenstein monster which is destroying the soul of its inventor. Materialism inevitably brings about the *Verdinglichung* of Marx, and, ultimately, the "reprobate sense" described by St. Paul. When man treats other men as beasts, he ends up by becoming one. So too when his world and all men in it are to him a machine, he ends up by becoming one.

But this is not the last of it. When the mystic looks upon every soul as a reflexion of God and sees all creation as His utterance, not only does he himself end up in the closer image and likeness of God, but he helps to bring mankind back to the original conception.

Though providing answers to almost all the questions which trouble the soul of man, the modern gospel is deficient in this one respect — that it gives a solution to none.

THEY DIDN'T LOOK AWAY

OLLOWING ONE ANOTHER IN the Stations of the Cross, the incidents connected first with Simon of Cyrene and then with Veronica have a relation to each other, and also to the general burden of this book.

When Simon left Cyrene for his visit to Jerusalem (which was probably an annual affair) the last thing he expected was that he should find himself taking part in the Passion. Whether he came to the capital for purposes of devotion, or for business reasons, or as part of a holiday, or in order to maintain his status as a Jew, it is certain that cross-carrying was no part of his original plan. Nor, very often, is it part of ours. Just as Simon was singled out by the Roman sergeant (almost fortuitously it would seem, but possibly because as a stranger from the provinces he would be less likely to resist and create a scene), so we are picked out, as it were from the crowd, to suffer. To the Roman soldiers, Simon was simply the nearest man, able-bodied and at the same time unrefusing, whom they could conveniently press into the service of the state. To God, Simon was that soul whose history hitherto had been a series of events leading up to this unique grace. Life is like that: outwardly the effect of mixed motives and unplanned circumstance, inwardly the manoeuvering into a pattern by the often unfelt directing influence of grace. Bring to the apparently chance happenings of our lives the supernatural light of faith and the whole scene changes. See things from God's angle, and what before was a narrow strip of flat horizon becomes a wide and varied skyline full of meaning and colour.

Simon of Cyrene symbolises for us the man in the street. Like ourselves he is one of the crowd. "God must be fond of ordinary people," said Abraham Lincoln, "or He wouldn't have made so many of them." Catherine Anne Emmerich, the ecstatic, says that Simon was a gardener by profession. If this was so it is further evidence that the humbler walks of life are often the most privileged. The most important family that the world has ever known consisted of a carpenter and his wife and her Child. It is fatally easy for us to think that unless we are possessed of unusual gifts or unless we are chosen for great undertakings we are of no account in the sight of God. "Everything about my life is so frightfully commonplace and ordinary and suburban that I can't fit it into the splendid picture of sanctity." A pair of nail-scissors does a very humble work and a radio-location set does a very difficult one, but you can't cut your nails with a radio-location set. It's all a question of what God wants you for.

Into Simon's prosaic and routine existence came, quite without warning, the summons to sacrifice. Not only quite without warning but quite without advertisement: it was manifested to him through the surprising channel of an unbelieving N. C. O. As a rustic provincial, Simon would have known little of the religious and political movements which had been stirring people's minds during the recent months in Jerusalem. It is unlikely that he would have known anything of the events which had led up to the affair in which he was now being involved. He had not yet fallen under the spell of our Lord's personality. Jesus Christ, to him, was just a name. The name of an agitator. Suddenly Simon finds himself carrying the gibbet of a condemned man. Even physically this must have been a severe test, but on other levels as well it cannot but have cost him a great deal to go through with it. The damage to his self-respect . . . the unwelcome publicity . . . the dread that the story would get out at home later on. But whether or not these considerations played a part in Simon's acceptance of the Cross, the point is that he accepted it — and accepted it, moreover, *not* at the hands of our Lord as might have been expected but at the hands of men. In some such apparently haphazard way do we become acquainted with the trials of our lives, and unless we go into the business with the will to receive everything, however unexpected and unpleasant, as it comes, we shall be in danger of either missing the chances that are offered us, or, when the chances are forced upon us, of being embittered by them. To the cross as to so much else can be applied the now familiar axiom "Whatever is received is received according to the dispositions of the recipient." It is not that we refuse the sufferings God sends us when we see that He is sending them, it is more that we fail to recognise them as coming from Him. Unless our crosses have got His name written all over them in block capitals they take us by surprise, and we resent their apparently meaningless interruption of our ordered lives. "It's so unreasonable." The cross is unreasonable — that's the whole point. Our lives are meant to be interrupted; our security is meant to be blown sky high by the meaningless; the calm surface of existence can't help being disturbed if there is to be any real reflexion of the Passion of Christ.

How, one wonders, did Simon respond? Did he, finding that the duty could not be avoided, accept the situation with a shrug of the shoulders? Or did he already know that the most satisfactory crosses were those which one had not oneself chosen? If it was with reluctance that he received the cross, then when did the change take place? As soon as his fingers touched the wood? Or did the sight of our Lord's patience work upon him — first upon his feelings, and then upon his inmost self? We don't know. Certainly by the time he was relieved of the weight he was a different person. He understood now the meaning of suffering: the meaning which had never quite emerged from the Old Law but which was now being unfolded for him in the New. Exhausted though he may have been from his share in bearing the weight of our Lord's cross, Simon must now have realised what a singular privilege was his — that he had been assisting in the penance of his Redeemer. What had looked like a humiliation had turned out to be an honour; what had been something to escape from was now something to meet with open arms. "I bear the marks of the Lord Jesus in my body," he could have said with St. Paul. It is surely not too fanciful to think of Simon in later years remembering with gratitude the events of this first Good Friday. Did he tell his grandchildren of the look which he had seen in the eyes of Christ? Of the joy which had flooded his soul on the discovery of what in his life had become most worth while? Of what he would have missed if somehow he had managed to evade the pressgang's summons? Glad should we be, with Simon of Cyrene, to bring to Christ a body ready for service and a will bent upon wasting nothing of its opportunity. Not only "shall every man bear his own burden" as St. Paul tells his Galatians, but by "bearing one another's also we shall" — as we learn from the same epistle — "fulfil the law of Christ."

In that episode in Christ's Passion which immediately followed the Simon incident we get an example of what at first sight appears to be much the same sort of thing — an act of charity rendering assistance to the Man of Sorrows — but which in fact was something very different. We link them together here because, as suggested above, they represent the grasping of the opportunity, the direct look of the unjaundiced eye.

All that we know about Veronica amounts to this: she was so deeply stirred by the sight of Christ's sufferings that she broke through the cordon of military which surrounded Him, and managed to get close enough to wipe away some of the blood and dirt from His face; the veil which she used for this purpose received a lasting imprint of our Lord's features, and became accordingly an object of the greatest veneration among the faithful. Veronica is numbered among the saints, though it is thought that this was not her name — "Vera ikon" deriving from the true likeness. which appeared upon the cloth which belonged to her. She is believed to have been the wife of an official in the capital, and later a great benefactress to the Church.

Unlike Simon's, Veronica's decision to help our Lord was completely spontaneous. This is the first thing about it, but it is not the most important. The most important thing about Veronica's magnificent act is that she managed to do it. Where Simon was rushed into the service of God, Veronica rushed herself into it. To her eternal credit it can be said that she kept up the rush. Sometimes we decide on the spur of the moment to do what we would never dream of doing if we sat down to think about it; if the thing is a good thing we must not allow ourselves time to go back on the decision, but, with Veronica blazing the trail for us, we must push the thing through and not sit down to think about it until afterwards.

Consider what Veronica was faced with when she stood on the crowded pavement of the narrow little street which today is called the Via Dolorosa. To any ordinary person it must have seemed out of the question that a sympathiser should be able to reach our Lord's side. There would be a scene; there would be an undignified scuffle in which a dishevelled woman might find herself arrested; the wife of an official would be in the news, would be laughed at, would have to defend her action; even if the thing were never to become public, there would have to be explanations in private to her friends and to her family; perhaps the condemned man for whose benefit the projected act was at this moment being turned over in her mind would never know who it was who had tried to come to his assistance. Was it worth it?

"Is it worth while having a shot at?" is a question which is so often followed by "I wonder if I really need?" that leaving the possible sequence of Veronica's thoughts out of consideration altogether we might profitably examine ourselves as to the point at which we begin to get out of things. We shall return to the Via Dolorosa in a minute; in the meantime what are the reasons which keep us back from possible acts of charity? Shame, surely, and laziness. The hesitancy which has us balancing until the moment has gone by is all too often due to the childish fear which nearly all of us grow up with — the fear of looking silly. We wonder what construction will be put upon our action, we doubt our ability to bring the thing off with dignity, we remember past failures under much the same sort of conditions, we wouldn't mind if we had time to plan our approach and decide exactly what attitude to strike....

Thus is the spontaneous response to grace suddenly frozen. Effort is paralysed; we turn to other things; the chance is missed. If only we were more objective in our charity we would be in less danger of thus hanging fire. If we thought more of the person to whom we were thinking of being charitable and less of the person who was thinking of it we would waste less time in being reflex. Once satisfied that grace is moving us to do something we should brush aside everything else and go ahead and do it. God is love: we have only to look at God in order to learn how to love. It is a mistake to examine the act of charity at the expense of charity's object. On the impulse of charity we have motive power enough for the greatest undertakings. And for the humblest undertakings no less. Nothing — least of all the thought of possible embarrassment or the thought of possible hardship — should keep us from what we conceive to be a project designed by God. When we think of the letters we might have written, of the calls we might have paid, of the invitations we might have accepted (and perhaps still more, sent), of the sympathetic things we might have said, of the offers we might have held out to people, when we think in short of the opportunities we have wasted *and why we have wasted them*, we blush with a shame which is far more disquieting than the shame which kept us from doing these things.

Now to get back to Veronica. Hers was exactly the attitude of mind which our Lord wanted to encourage in His hearers when He told the story of the good Samaritan. "Don't look away." What a consolation it must have been to Him in that dark hour to have seen Veronica breaking magnificently through the ring of soldiers that surrounded Him. He knew that what might have remained in Veronica's heart as no more than a wave of pity had in fact grown into a great demonstration of praise. You may call it an impetuous gesture if you like, but it is evidently the kind of impetuous gesture that God values. If it is born of an emotion, it is at least born of a dynamic emotion, and not a sterile one. It is symptomatic; if it is a flourish, it is a significant flourish. Watch her as she charges in among the men from the shelter of her wall, and sweeps the veil off her head. Watch her as she holds out the cloth to receive the head of Christ. The crowd, meanwhile, falling back from sheer astonishment, are wondering what will happen next. Gingerly at first, and then with increasing pressure, she draws the soft material over the broken skin . . . slowly she wipes the grime from the cheekbones, chin, and neck . . . gently she smooths the caked and matted hair. It was worth it; she hadn't looked away. They could arrest her *now* if they liked: it was the possibility of having to leave off half way that had tried to stop her. Friends will gossip?

People will cut her in the street? She won't be invited to people's houses? Her name will be remembered in society on account of that sudden infatuation for a prisoner? She will be bracketed (quite correctly in the event) with Mary Magdalen? Nothing matters: she has done her act of charity and has had her reward; God will look after the rest. She has staked a good deal, and she has won. If there is an incidental price to pay she can meet it.

The lesson of all this, then, is to look for Christ where He can be found — at no more than perhaps a moment's notice and under the most unlikely appearance. "Thy face, O Lord, will I seek," we can say with the Psalmist, and we must remember at the same time that His face will not always be beautiful: with humanity He is wounded from head to foot until there is no soundness in Him. The Man of Sorrows is not always to be discovered under the most inviting disguises. We must not expect to get any thrill from ministering to the members of His Mystical Body, but it will be just as real a service as any that was rendered to the members of His actual body. It is for us to assume with the conviction of faith that whoever presents himself before us as a possible object of our charity is in fact the representative — as surely as the impression which was left upon Veronica's veil was the representation — of Christ. It is for us to cultivate that lost-property-office mentality which receives indiscriminately whatever comes along, whether battered and broken or in good condition. Human driftwood is plentiful enough, but all too few are those who stand on the shore ready to gather it up. The sick and the poor are not the only ones deserving of our charity; there are the snubbed, the strayed, the left behind, the lonely. There are also those who may not deserve our charity but who nevertheless require it: the impostors, the ungrateful, the tiresome people who make capital out of the generosity of others, the thrusters, the bores, the thoughtless. The more it costs us to display our charity, the more directly is it a charity done to Christ. If it costs us our comfort it is far from worthless; if it costs us our time and energy it is better still; if it costs us something in the way of shame and shyness it is certainly leading us in the way of the saints; if it costs us our reputation it is best of all. If Veronica had thought more about her reputation than about her love, one of the most splendid incidents in history would have been lost to us, and the Church would have had to go without a saint. As it is we have the knowledge that much must be risked — a good name among other things — in the exercise of the most Christian virtue, and we have also in heaven a patron of the shy and self-conscious who can pray that in their projected acts of charity souls may be more aware of Christ than of themselves.

THE ENDS OF CHAPTERS

"THE WORST PART ABOUT BEING on the shelf is not so much having to drop one's contacts," a priest once said to me, "as having to try and keep them up." The meaning of this rather bloodless statement became clear in subsequent conversation. For some years he had been employed in a work which had brought him in close touch with souls, and this work had suddenly been taken away from him. From a distance he had watched the progress of the same work under his successor, and every now and then had gone back to meet the friends to whom he had given the best years of his life. At these return visits he found that what he had expected to be current topics were not current topics, that references had to be explained, that news had to be brought up-to-date, that an almost different idiom had come into fashion, and that the consequent effort on both sides to bridge the gap was making for discomfort and strain. The account of all this to me ended with the expected and miserably lonely phrase: "The truth is that I'm out of it." The spell had been broken.

The drawback to being relieved of duty is not of course that one feels out of it but that one still feels in it. Indeed the whole process of increasing years would lose its dread if one could only manage to grow old; the horror is not that one is past it but that one isn't.

The loneliness of not *having* to think of other people is one of the evils of retirement which are never foreseen.

In almost any work there is the necessity, and in most works the obligation, of taking an interest in other people's interests and of looking at things from other people's points of view. When this comes suddenly to an end we recognise the poverty of our own interests and the limitations of our view. This is humbling and salutary, but it clears the way for a quite undisputed selfishness. With no one else to worry about, self can become the supreme arbiter in everything. Proverbially self-opinionated, self-centred, self-pitying are those no longer in the whirl of active work. The dangers are all the greater where retirement has come prematurely and not voluntarily. One feels like a Moses with forty years and a wilderness before him, and no chosen people to lead. The adventure has died; the wilderness is arid; the future is not to be thought of. It is now that previous training in the spiritual life is going to come to the rescue. Until new contacts are worked up — and unless there are very good signs to the contrary they should be worked up, even at the cost of great effort — God is the only refuge. This is precisely why He has shaken us out of our settled course and allowed our lives to be broken up: so that we should look to Him. He has told us that He is our support, yet we insist on supporting ourselves; He has told us that He is our consolation, yet we insist on providing our own. Not that God is necessarily punishing us for the amount of self that was found in our work, but simply that He wants us kept supple, kept on the move, prevented from hardening into any sort of mould. We have to be always yielding to Him, always ready to lean on Him, and an occasional jolt which shatters the framework of our lives is probably just what we need: it brings us back from independence to dependence. We are on a string, and to be jerked back every now and then reminds us of it.

What we have seen earlier on in this book as regards creatures applies here with regard to occupations. It is the story of the Israelites over again. Never settling down; constant uprootings; change, change, change. We take our sleep when we can get it, we eat standing up, we roll up our tents before dawn. No lasting city; even the oasis we must be ready to leave at a moment's notice. "Nothing endureth," says Ecclesiastes wistfully, "under the sun." The sun-dial can't be put back. The show goes on. There may be other oases in front of us . . . or again there may not. God can be left to arrange all that. In any case the halt will be only for a time. Heavens, why do we desert pilgrims make such a scene when the sand gets into the omelette and that jolly little village over there turns out to be a mirage after all?

Much of life's bitterness would be spared us if we learned how to let go gracefully. People who are supposed to be surrendered to the will of God should not have to wait until their fingers one by one have been forced back from their grasp. Yet the best of us cling on. Not only to jobs, but to things and people and happiness and, inordinately perhaps, to life.

> *How can she catch the sunlight*
> *And bind it in her hair?*
> *Where is the golden apple*
> *Whose core is not despair?*
> *How shall one cull the honey*
> *And yet not rob the flower?*
> *And who may say he's happy*
> *In the passing of the hour?**

The trouble is that though we may know beyond all doubt, and as the melancholy result of experience, that the sunlight cannot be caught and that eating golden apples is a desperate business anyway, and so on all along the line, there *still* exist such excellent reasons why some things should be clung to and not given up without a struggle. We are the only people who know how to handle them; we are the people who have built the whole thing up from scratch and can be trusted to finish the work properly; there is waste of energy and opportunity all round if we are not given a free hand

---

* I regret that I am unable to trace the authorship of this verse, and am thus unable to ask permission to quote it here. Rather than leave it out, I acknowledge my gratitude in these terms and trust that the presumption may be pardoned. Also, having relied upon my memory, the exact wording may be incorrect.

at this particular moment; when a work is entrusted to us by God it is our duty to fight tooth and nail to keep charge of it. We say these things and perhaps we believe them, but of course they are sheer nonsense really. Pride underlies the entire list: confidence in our own ability and lack of confidence in God's. Besides, if obedience removes a certain work from us — even if it is the obedience which is dictated to us through circumstance — that settles it. What is it that hurts us most when we are relieved from the care of souls? Putting it at its highest, is it not the fear that those who have been helped by us will find help from no one else and so will be in danger: This is a terrible fear; it plays upon the imagination, and we see souls tumbling into hell because we are unable to come to the rescue. It is an idle fear nevertheless. It comes straight from an exaggerated idea of our own influence and a complete want of trust in God's providence. Nothing is being wasted: if He removes us, and so allows chaos to prevail in outward affairs and danger to threaten inward ones, then it is not beyond His power to bring order out of chaos and triumph out of trial. Every sympathy to the man who sees the work which he has fashioned with his own hand given into the hands of another. He feels as Noe might have felt if he had been asked at the last moment to get out and swim: it's no fun for him, while floating about in the rain and gathering gloom outside, to see what is going on through the lighted windows of the ark which he has made. All sympathy to him certainly, but let him not talk of waste. Nothing in this is wasted — save possibly the opportunity of seeing in these affairs the designs of God. Far from his own talents being wasted they are being worked, but not in the way that appeals to him. There are times when we don't mind seeing our talent buried, because we feel there is something humble in the process, and we know that if the worst comes to the worst we can always dig it up again; nor do we mind seeing our talent drawn upon, because we know that this is what it is for; the thing we object to is seeing it left on the side of the road, because then it means that no one values it. This is the time to pick it up again and put it to a new use. Presumably God still values it.

THE SHOW GOES ON

N THE MORNING BEFORE the first performance of a certain play in London, the entire staff of stage hands came out on strike. Others were engaged and instructed in their duties. During the dress rehearsal that afternoon the leading lady collapsed on the stage and had to be rushed off to a nursing home where she underwent a serious operation a few hours later. Her understudy was sent for and took over the part. An emergency rehearsal was called next morning, and while this was going on the lighting throughout the house fused, and, because it was found to be dangerous, the whole system had to be rewired. Hearing that several members of the cast were expressing uneasiness about the production of the play that evening and were wondering whether a postponement might not under the circumstances be a good thing, the producer assembled the company in the stalls and addressed them (from the still lifeless footlights) thus: "Rather than leave you in doubt about the date of our first night, I think you should know that if the scenery catches fire before the curtain goes up, if the roof falls in during the opening dialogue, if the hero is struck down in the storm scene by real lightning, and if the author has to re-write the last act during the interval between the first and second, *the show goes on*." And in fact it did.

In the preceding essay we considered the way in which we should relinquish; here we consider the way in which we should retain. As a general principle it is safe to say that unless obedience or the signified will of God intervenes we go on with the thing in hand until we drop. This idea raises no less than four separate problems: Obedience, outside the religious life, can be elastic; how is it to be interpreted? The will of God is variously signified; what are the indications to be acted upon? The thing in hand may refer equally to a hobby or to earning a livelihood; which is intended? Lastly, when have we reached the stage designated by the words "until we drop"? A paragraph may be devoted to each of these questions.

Obedience, where there is no vow to define its terms, is taken here to be the serious wish of any authority which is not manifestly unjustified. The serious wish, be it noted, and not only the expressed command. Thus all legitimate superiors — whether in the army, the hospital, the school, the office, and so on — can tell us to stop doing what we are doing or tell us to do it in a different way. But if they do not tell us to stop, or, more absolutely, tell us not to stop, we go on until we drop. The borderline obedience is that which is owed to doctors and spiritual directors. I am myself of the opinion (and this in no way commits any one besides myself) that so long as the medical advice is of our own seeking we are not strictly bound to follow it. If we don't agree, or if a higher principle is involved, we pay the man's bill and look for someone else. (Or, better still, carry on without looking for someone else.) So also in the case of the spiritual director: provided he deals with us on a take-it-or-leave-it basis we are free to brush his opinion aside. But if we are told, in the first instance, to act on the doctor's orders, and, in the second, to accept the ruling of a certain director, we have to obey. In either case we are under new and particular obligations. But unless we are forbidden by obediences of such a sort as we have just described to continue with what we are engaged upon, we go on with it until we drop.

The will of God is indicated for us, where it isn't indicated by authority, in the circumstances which come to shape our lives. A war, an illness, a financial collapse would be the sorts of indication to consider. Obviously if the cause for which the work was being done is removed, then there is nothing to be gained by going on with it. The will of God is that it should stop. There is the tendency, however, to see the signified will of God in what is entirely insignificant. Before laying down a work it is as well to remember that God normally signifies His will by giving us the grace to go on doing it.

Of the four clauses, the most slippery of interpretation is the one to do with "the thing in hand." As far as work goes, clearly we have to do it for as long as it lasts — come what may. But there is so much else besides work which we embark upon and then get tired of and want to drop. There are our Lenten penances, there is our voluntary correspondence, there are our devotional practices, our not strictly necessary labours, our charities, our hospitalities, our social duties and activities. The solution here is surely to find out in prayer or by taking advice what is the particular line which God wants to see pursued, and then not allow anything in the world to interfere with the pursuit of it. Unless (again) stopped by obedience, the course is stuck to. You may lose money, you may lose prestige, you may lose position, and health, and friends, but if you go on doing what you have reason to believe that God wants you to do, you will not be the loser in the end.

Fourthly and finally, by the words "until we drop" is meant quite simply that we do not give in until we drop. The show goes on.

HOLY SATURDAY

IT IS A CURIOUS FACT THAT only when we are asleep and dreaming do we get anywhere near to the reality of a previous experience. Memory, when we are awake, takes us some of the way, but we have to be in the unreal world of dreams and nightmares before we can re-live in any real sense the emotions of the past. "You remember what it felt like during the war," people say. But of course you can't. You know now what happened next. It is only when you don't know what happened next that you can recall the quality of what time and altered circumstances have made remote. Say you are dreaming that you are sitting for an examination which in actual fact you have passed (or failed) long ago, you do then experience the precise sensations of anxiety and doubt and hope and effort which stirred you as you stared at the question paper. But in the ordinary way you can't *remember* what it was like. Once you have got the key to any situation it is impossible to imagine the situation without it. That's why it's a mistake to read the last chapter of a detective story first. What childhood was really like might conceivably be remembered by a madman, because a madman might conceivably have forgotten everything else. But it can't be remembered by a sane person, because a sane person knows the sequence. To experience the enchantment of youth you have either to be asleep or mad—or young.

God has no need to remember things; we have. And with us the trouble is that, apart from the cases already mentioned, we never quite can. This is because we have got finite minds, and can't help seeing everything as happening in a series. By the time one minute arrives the one before has ceased to be, and because it has ceased to be it can't be recaptured at a future date unless all the intervening minutes have been taken out of the way. So effectively sometimes are the intervening minutes taken out of the way in a dream that all sorts of accidental qualities are revived: not only is the authentic thrill of climbing over a wall at night, for instance, experienced all over again but one actually feels as fit and agile as one did then, and one fears and enjoys the things which would now no longer cause us fear and joy. The moment we wake up we have got the key again, and the spell is broken.

Thus when we try and enter into the spirit of the liturgy, we are, when we come to Holy Saturday, at a disadvantage. We can't even remotely understand what it felt like to be one of the disciples when our Lord was in the tomb, because we know what happened next. We have been given the keys; we have been let out. To us whose whole hope hangs upon the sequel, the events of Good Friday and Holy Saturday fit in. Holy Week is of a piece; everything adds up with what has gone before and with what will be explained as the story is yet to be unfolded. For us it is impossible to isolate any one day in the history of the Passion, or even in the whole Gospel record, and to think of it as apart from its answer and explanation, Easter Sunday.

But because we cannot fully appreciate the disciples' sense of hopelessness it doesn't mean that the significance of Holy Saturday is therefore lost to us. The point of following the events commemorated in the Church's calendar is not to provide occasions of guessing at other people's sentiments but to provide occasions of canalising and supernaturalising our own. The particular force of Holy Saturday lies, as we shall see in a minute, in the encouragement which it gives to those who are being tempted to despair. Perhaps this is why the older we get the more our lives tend to hang upon the thought of the Resurrection. For most of us it is Christmas that is our favourite feast at the beginning; in the end we know the need of Easter.

The Gospel account, like the liturgical cycle, is an invitation to us to come and, in the measure of each man's generosity, do likewise. To enable us to respond to this appeal we are given the *whole* Gospel story, the *whole* liturgical cycle, with the Resurrection as the climax and fulfilment. It is as well we are. Religion is difficult enough for most of us without our being stuck for ever between Good Friday and Easter Sunday. With the knowledge of Easter Sunday in our minds we can see the meaning of "Lose your life and you will save it," of "the seed must die first before it bring forth fruit," of the whole Gospel principle regarding self-surrender.

It is because we know that it is not the end that we poor feeble creatures can join with the souls of greater spirit who, during the first Holy Week, rolled the stone to the mouth of the sepulchre. Did Joseph of Arimathea expect a Resurrection? Did Nicodemus? Did even John? We don't know. Certainly when they buried their Lord they must have buried with Him many of their hopes as well. Our closeness to the buried Christ, informed as such a mental attitude must inevitably be by the knowledge of what was to follow, should give us what we need to fight discouragement and disappointment. For those who are called upon to watch the frittering away of powers which they might under other circumstances be using for the glory of God there is material for thought in the burial of Christ. Even Herodotus recognised the supreme mortification of finding no outlet for the exercise of useful energy: ἐχθίστη ὀδυνὴ τῶν ἐν ἀνθρώποις αὕτη he makes his Theban say, πολλὰ φρονέοντα μηδενὸς κρατέειν — hope deferred, effort misdirected, the sands running out and nothing to show for it. Life which looked at one time like being such a great success turns out to be a complete flat failure. Now is the time to practise faith; now is the time to hold to the doctrine that there need never be any waste unless we choose to allow it. It is in the dark that we have more than ever to keep our eyes open, and there is no darkness like the silent gloom of the sepulchre of Christ. Those who have had their plans shattered, their enterprises stifled, their achievements crowned by muddle, and their proffered help rejected, should find much to console them in the fourteenth Station of the Cross, much to look forward to in the thought of the risen Christ. "Your life is hid with Christ in God," says St. Paul to the Colossians. "When Christ shall appear who is your life," he adds, "then you also will appear with Him in glory."

There is much to be said for the hidden life — whether before or after or instead of the active life — but it is not always clear that it is "with Christ in God." The temptation is to feel that one isn't really living at all, that one might just as well be dead with Christ in the tomb. This is sheer delusion. The vocation to be *absconditus in Deo*, even if it is only for a time, means that active co-operation with the Passion is being replaced by a co-operation that is passive. Nothing is being lost; it is merely being less obvious. In fact there is probably a gain: the contemplative act is higher than that of the active. The idea is that we have to work in the open for as long as we can, and then, when for one reason or another we are pushed into a cave, we have to switch over from one operation to another: we go on working but in a different key. The switch-over is bound to be uncomfortable. One of the things we have to get used to is not being leant upon. To want to be felt necessary to people is a far greater luxury, though a far more subtle one, than the desire to lean on them. In the hidden life there is no scope for this particular self-indulgence. In the hidden life the soul is cut off not only very often from actual association, but — and this is much more searching — from the sight of any fruit of its labour. Faith is required to go on with a work which is so designed as to bring with it no sense of achievement. It feels utterly pointless. That's the point. Holy Saturday in the sepulchre is the answer: shut away from the racket of the capital . . . waiting the revelation of a richer and more real life . . . in the meantime blackness, loneliness, apparent frustration, cold . . . the body of Jesus present indeed, but absent the consolation of seeing Him as present.

OUR LADY'S SORROWS

MERCIFULLY WE ARE allowed for the most part to forget our sorrows and to remember our joys. We even find it hard to compare—if we are foolish enough to waste time in trying to compare—one sorrow with another. The past seems to obscure our powers of valuation. Each suffering that comes along has a way of eclipsing anything that has been experienced before. It is not necessarily that the suffering is worse or that we have grown more sensitive; it is simply that we have forgotten. God has wanted us to face this new trial with a mind untroubled by the thought of what it felt like last time. He knows that if our sorrows were to linger with us with all the weight with which other experiences have lingered with us, we should be so weighed down as to be useless from the point of view of further endurance. It is humiliating to realise that we are possessed of such a slender store of generosity that God has to wipe away the memory of one suffering before He can comfortably entrust us with another.

Often after a more than ordinary upset, we find ourselves saying: "Well, nothing can ever be as bad as this again . . . there's at least the comfort of knowing that I've touched rock bottom at last." We say the same when the next blow falls. The truth is we don't know what rock bottom is; we have not the least idea as to the capacity which we have for suffering; previous experience — except in so far as the suffering has been the same in character — provides no measurement. Like falling in love, and genius, and the sunrise, it is a new thing every time.

We get so accustomed to the way in which the unpleasant interludes of life hurry one another along without leaving any very noticeable traces that on the rare occasions when a sorrow obstinately refuses to heal we are puzzled; we even put it down to religion, and imagine that God is not taking the trouble to tidy up our lives for us as He used to do, and as He appears to do for other people. We resent the fact that the burden of the cross seems to grow heavier instead of lighter as time goes on. We begin to wonder whether perhaps God is not singling us out for harsh treatment; we decide that possibly we are one of those rare victim souls who are meant to live out their time in shadow and not in sunshine. We sink into a slime of self-pity. Much better, surely, to humble ourselves and admit that our powers of endurance are so slender that only once in a way does a suffering stay behind, when all of them, had we been more perfect and more generous, might have been allowed by God to assume a permanency in our lives. The cross is so much part of perfection that to the perfect it is never very far away. To the really perfect, like our Lady, every cross is so much more of a reality than it is to us that it does not fade out of the picture when the new one is painted in. It is not that holy people cling to their crosses, deriving a melancholy satisfaction from them when they are there and treasuring their memory when they are over; it is much more that holy people are permitted to endure sorrow on the same principle that the rest of us are permitted to enjoy pleasure: the saints suffer more of the pain because they have come, with the development of grace in their souls, to see more of its meaning. Pain and memory are not two things, but one. Pain is renewed when it is recalled; it is the same pain, not a different one. Indeed until a pain has dwelled in the mind and been remembered, it hasn't really been suffered. The saints are those who are so privileged as to be able, without either a morbid interest or a desire to sit among the ruins, to retain in the mind such sufferings as the pace of their progress demands. No fanatic cult of pain on the one hand or flight on the other. The saint is what a French writer has called a *résigné aventureux*, a man who looks his lot in the face—whether it comes to him as a kick or a caress.

Why should we, after all, resent the more tenacious sorrows? We do not think it peculiar that joys should settle down as part of our lives. Why should it be different in the case of grief? Memory *must* be part of each. How else could any sustained effect be produced? It isn't the shock of the cross, it's living with it that sanctifies. Surely everyone is able to point to a certain sorrow in his life which, though it may not have lasted more than two minutes when it was turned full on, has grown into the background of his life in a way which others have not done. The immediate wound, the stab of it, was over in no time; it was the hurt which stopped on. Here, in its survival, is its real meaning; in today is its significance to be found; the three minutes of blinding agony were only the beginning, and of themselves easy enough to get over. The pain was meant then, but means much more now.

Simeon told our Lady in the Temple that a sword would pierce her heart. In the event her heart was pierced by seven swords — and indeed by many more besides. I wonder if it is stretching the text too far to see in St. Luke's references to Mary's "keeping all these things, pondering them in her heart" the inclusion of many lasting sorrows at once. If popular devotion is any indication, then certainly the familiar representation of our Lady with the seven swords bears out what has been suggested. Where we, in those rare instances when a sword runs through us, tug so constantly at the blade and scream so piteously for mercy that God withdraws the pain, Mary, more exposed to suffering than any living being apart from her Son, took to herself the sorrows of mankind and kept them, pondering them in her heart together with the sufferings of our Lord.

THE GOOD NEWS OF THE GOSPEL

BEFORE THE COMING OF CHRIST there was, for those who wanted it, virtue in abundance. The pagans were all in favour of justice and prudence and self-control and perseverance. These, they said, were reasonable: the complete man had need of them. Then came Christ and gave us faith, hope, and charity; which, as He interpreted them and as judged by pagan acceptations, were unreasonable virtues. The whole point of the theological virtues is that they go on when the ordinary apparatus of the mind has had to give up. We continue to believe when we feel there's no sense in going on with it: when we don't feel that faith is there any more. We hope when all reasonable grounds for hope have ceased to have any meaning for us: we hope because we have faith in its reality. We love on, not because we feel like it or even because people deserve to be loved, but simply because we know that if charity stops there is nothing else left. It is a curious catalogue of essential virtues which depends for its exercise upon expressions which have nothing in the least to do with feeling virtuous. The Gospel message was certainly something new.

"A new commandment I give unto you." But hadn't the Greeks got it? Weren't they urged to be merciful and hospitable and so on? Yes, but Christ came with a precept, not merely with a counsel. Christ extended the field of its operation until there were absolutely no limits whatever. You must love as your heavenly Father loves . . . the worthless as much as the worthy . . . forgiving not seven times but seventy times seven times . . . and if you don't do this it isn't that eventually you will find that your love of God suffers, it is that you are not as a fact loving God now. Salvation depends upon it.

It must have been staggering to our Lord's generation to learn that salvation depended upon something so unreasonable as loving the people whom you didn't like. The love of God is reasonable, but is the love of man? And yet you pass from death to life by practising it. Though God and the Church enlist the services of reason, they do on occasion ask of their subjects the unreasonable. Never what is against reason, but often what is beyond it. It is then that we on our side, so as to get out of doing what is wanted of us, call reason to witness the justice of our claims. We make reason an excuse, and so smother our consciences. There are many borderline cases where we can find reasons for doing things for which there is often no excuse. What does this mean? It means that we have left the Gospel level and have slid back on common sense. "I can't reasonably be expected to . . ." Of course not, but supernaturally you can, and you've been given the grace to. "There are excellent reasons for believing that this will turn out to everyone's advantage, and since no one is likely to suffer harm, I think on this occasion we are justified in . . . " There may be good reasons, but that doesn't say that there are good motives. We shall not be judged upon the reasons which we have invented, but upon the motives on which we have acted. Love can be asked to leapfrog reasons; it is its motives that give it pace. "Heroism urges and never reasons," says Emerson, "and therefore is always right." Has any saint, hovering on the edge of a decision, asked himself whether the proposed course of action was in keeping with what mankind at large would judge as being reasonable?

The good news of the Gospel included three pieces of information that were startling in their novelty. The first instructed mankind in the need to transcend the normal, the accepted, the practical, the material, and to look at the things which neither sense nor reason could comprehend. The second stated a fact, and demanded that the guarantees which accompanied it should be adhered to with confidence in spite of whatever appeared to the contrary. The third said, unequivocally, love.

WE LIVE WITH OUR EYES OPEN

HERE IS A QUOTATION FROM Joubert: "How many people eat, drink, marry, buy, sell, build, make fortunes, acquire friends and enemies, enjoy pleasure, endure pain; in short are born, grow up and die—but asleep." It is this sleep that the present work is designed to counter. A concluding essay, therefore, may suitably be devoted to roping in the salient points in the essays that have gone before, and viewing them in the light of the open eye.

First and most obviously there is the necessity of looking at life with a challenging hope. To those who expect much of life, life brings even more. "What is received, is received according to the measure of the recipient"—and overflowing. With a love that, far from being blind, is penetrating in its vision, we look at people and causes for the best they have to offer, not the worst. No facile optimism is this, nor a devotion that refuses to face the faults and flaws; it is simply the realism of the idealist who sees what is wrong and how capable it is of right. The fanatic, whether his energies are directed in favour of or against an existing order, is a very different person from the idealist. In the half light they may look the same, but where one is an eccentric who thrives on the excess of his own zest, the other is an enthusiast who forgets about his personality in his effort to realise his principle.

Again, to look on life with open eyes is to leave aside the unreal and make direct for the real. It is to search out the true, the essential as God made it, and not to be deflected by the near-true, the accidental, the glamorous. There are many who labour under the disability of being always attracted by the part rather than by the whole, by the irrelevant rather than by the significant. The kind of man who in playing tennis prefers the shot to the game, who in literature prefers the words to the ideas they clothe, who in art prefers the artistry to the forms it represents, is likely when it comes to the more vital things in life to stop short at the covering and be perfectly ready to accept the standard valuation. Not only does he shelve the responsibility of thinking and looking for himself — taking what other people have thought and seen as being good enough for him — but even when he uses his faculties and interests himself in the life that is going on all around him he leaves off at the point where the thing becomes really worth while. There are some who seem to be interested in everything about people except the people themselves. This is especially the danger for those who have the care of souls. Indeed for them there is the further danger, as a result of having to talk much of spirituality, of making the same mistake on an even higher plane: they can become expert in everything connected with the service of God, and forget about God Himself. There is no doubt about it, the care of souls opens up innumerable possibilities — either way.

There may be people who open their eyes too wide, and who see so much that nothing is related; certainly these are to be preferred to those who are too lazy to look. Better to see everything and see it badly, than not to bother if it's there or not. What most of us need to cultivate is the innocent eye which is not ashamed to open in wonder. When our ability to wonder is exhausted, when our curiosity is no longer operating, then is the time to take ourselves seriously in hand. The too enquiring mind is obviously more of a liability than an asset; but the mind which is too listless to enquire might just as well not exist at all. Hardly surprising that Christ so often gave us children as our models: to the child there is nothing commonplace, nothing which cannot be vested with some sort of interest. Even if we can't welcome the normal with a glad cry of surprise, there is no reason why we should deny it the beauty which belongs to it. Beauty jumps out of the dustbin if you let it. Those who are ready to be dazzled by the everyday are not only happier and holier than those who are deadened by the drab, but they are also far easier to get on with. What is it that makes people dreary companions? What is it that makes them stimulating? Not their intelligences, their secret sorrows, their outward circumstances; these are so many accidents. What really tells is the use they make of opportunity. Let a man find adventure in his back garden, but don't let him think that adventure can exist nowhere else. Life, beauty, reality are everywhere.

> *The sin I impute to each frustrate ghost*
> *Is the unlit lamp and the ungirt loin.*

This is the degradation, this is where the waste comes in. We should be on fire to make use of every chance that comes along. We allow so much to pass us by which might be swept up into the service of God: sufferings come into our lives, but somehow as possible offerings to be made to God they slip through our fingers; people come into our lives but as souls to receive the impress of Christ they are somehow overlooked; works, pleasures, undertakings of one kind and another come crowding into our lives, but somehow in the general rush are accepted in their own terms — materially. The great work of supernaturalisation goes untried. And all the time, while neglecting the sanctification-value of what lies immediately before us, we are straining with a very undivine discontent to break through the ring of circumstance with which the will of God surrounds us. There is need here, lest we miss the inwardness of our outward lives, to keep our eyes well open to the light.

Right relations with God, with people, with oneself: life is no more than this, and no less. Love is the secret with regard to God and man, honesty with regard to self. Our love of God is conditioned and measured by our faith: if with the eye of faith we see the meaning, we have no need to hunger for the feeling. The soul who looks to the will, and lays it alongside that of Christ dwelling within, has nothing to worry about as regards devotion.

No less than in our dealings with God, it is the will that regulates our dealings with people. We love man if we choose to love, we don't if we exclude him. Feelings are no index to our charity. And where it is a question of the affections — love in the particular and personal sense — the same principle has its application: look to the meaning of love, and leave its emotion to come over and above its right use. As happiness is to life, so pleasure is to love: each to be found in its proper element but not to be looked for as an entity by itself. The essential is the life: the essential is the love. Miss out the essential and the rest crumbles to dust in your hand.

Finally: honesty towards oneself. Blessed is the man who can look his own image, as God sees it, in the face and say: "Here am I." Without pride he must see himself as being capable of doing great things for God. Without ambition he must see himself as being able to give a lead to men. In either direction he must prepare himself to meet and overcome disappointment; only so can his fidelity be of any value at all. In his service of God he must remember that he is neither directing nor doing a favour. In his leadership of man he must remember that he is ministering and not monopolising.

He must respect his following, not repress it. Nothing whip-lash in his approach, nothing which exacts more than what is there to give. He must be himself, and accept whatever answer comes from man. There may be no answer, in which case he humbles himself and goes on with his life, as best he can, alone. The same if for a time God gives him a following and then takes it away again: he humbles himself and gets on alone as before. It will leave him more time to be himself with God. Archbishop Goodier once said in a retreat (and the words might have been applied to himself): "The mark of a leader is to be able to withdraw himself from his work when the time comes without either imperilling the work or crushing his own spirit: the work and the man go on. The work goes on living the life he gave to it, the man goes on with another but no less fruitful work in solitude. The leader, when the hour of retirement arrives, detaches his work from himself in the same way that nature detaches a ripe fruit from the tree." In that retirement also when a man comes, with his eyes open, to meet death, there should be this same detachment of the spirit. Leaders may be rare, but men are not. A man may let his life fall from him like an apple ... knowing that it has been a windfall all along.

ABOUT THE CENACLE PRESS
AT SILVERSTREAM PRIORY

An apostolate of the Benedictine monastery of Silverstream Priory in Ireland, the mission of The Cenacle Press can be summed up in four words: *Quis ostendit nobis bona* — who will show us good things (Psalm 4:6)? In an age of confusion, ugliness, and sin, our aim is to show something of the Highest Good to every reader who picks up our books. More specifically, we believe that the treasury of the centuries-old Benedictine tradition and the beauty of holiness which has characterised so many of its followers through the ages has something beneficial, worthwhile, and encouraging in it for every believer.

cenaclepress.com

ALSO AVAILABLE:

Dom Hubert Van Zeller
We Die Standing Up (paper)
We Sing while there's Voice Left (paper)
We Live with Our Eyes Open (paper)
Letters to A Soul

Blessed Columba Marmion
Christ the Ideal of the Monk
Christ in His Mysteries
Words of Life On the Margin of the Missal

Robert Hugh Benson
The King's Achievement
By What Authority
The Friendship of Christ
Christ in the Church
Confessions of a Convert

Visit cenaclepress.com
for our full catalogue.

www.ingramcontent.com/pod-product-compliance
Lightning Source LLC
Chambersburg PA
CBHW030258100526
44590CB00012B/435